Palgrave Studies in the History of Economic Thought

Palgrave Studies in the History of Economic Thought publishes contributions by leading scholars, illuminating key events, theories and individuals that have had a lasting impact on the development of modern-day economics. The topics covered include the development of economies, institutions and theories.

More information about this series at
http://www.palgrave.com/gp/series/14585

Pervez Tahir

Making Sense of Joan Robinson on China

palgrave
macmillan

Pervez Tahir
Islamabad, Pakistan

ISSN 2662-6578 ISSN 2662-6586 (electronic)
Palgrave Studies in the History of Economic Thought
ISBN 978-3-030-28824-2 ISBN 978-3-030-28825-9 (eBook)
https://doi.org/10.1007/978-3-030-28825-9

Cover illustration: Archive PL / Alamy Stock Photo

This Palgrave Macmillan imprint is published by the registered company Springer Nature Switzerland AG.
The registered company address is: Gewerbestrasse 11, 6330 Cham, Switzerland

Preface (2020)

Around the start of 2018, Geoff Harcourt encouraged me to send a proposal to Laura Pacey at Palgrave Macmillan to publish this volume. It was written during my stint as Joan Robinson Memorial Lecturer at the Faculty of Economics, University of Cambridge in 1990. Some earlier work was done as part of my doctoral work at Cambridge, supervised by Geoff. In the original dissertation completed and submitted in 1988, "Making Sense of Joan Robinson on China" was a three-page appendix. The main essay was on Joan Robinson in princely India of the late 1920s. In a letter to the Director of Research at the Faculty, her husband, Sir Austin Robinson, claimed that the work I attributed to Joan Robinson was actually his. I believed I had enough evidence to support my contention. However, in deference to Sir Austin (remember, the Faculty building is named after him), the committee asked me to revise the dissertation.

I had never known Joan Robinson personally. She had passed away before I came up to Selwyn College in 1984. My college time in Lahore, Pakistan, coincided with the heady days of the 1960s. Students everywhere in the world were revolting against the established order. Like many others, Mao was our ideal. I had enjoyed reading *Freedom and Necessity* and *The Cultural Revolution in China*. So as a young man, I was a lot more starry-eyed than Joan Robinson! At the University of Colorado at Boulder in 1980–81, an arch Post-Keynesian, Tracy Mott, exposed me further to the continuity of thought in Marx, Keynes, Kalecki and Joan Robinson. I was able to tell the "bastard Keynesians" from others. Regardless, the reason to choose Joan Robinson as the subject of my dissertation was different.

I had left the country because of the suffocation I felt during the obscurantist and fascistic regime of General Zia ul Haq. I thought it was a good time to complete my education. But I did not want to do any empirical work that might require going back home to collect data or carry out fieldwork. A few meetings with Geoff led to the decision to work on the development-related work of Joan Robinson. In August 1988, the military regime ended after General Zia's death in a plane crash. Instead of revising my dissertation, I left for Pakistan.

Geoff had not given up on me, though. Not only did he prevail on me to return and revise the dissertation, he and John Sender, my internal examiner, induced me to explore in depth Joan Robinson's forays into China. Peter Nolan, my official Faculty Adviser, challenged me no end. Other doctoral candidates were all too willing to help in any way they could. I remember Masood Karshenas, Andy Mckay, Anjali, Additiya Mattoo and a nice couple from Sri Lanka. This is how a three-page appendix developed into a long essay. Geoff must have liked it enough to rope in Prue to bring out a shorter version in 2002.[1] Thirty years on, its publication was not easy. When Geoff asked me to submit the manuscript to Palgrave Macmillan, I discovered to my horror that I had misplaced my copy. Yet again, Geoff went scouting. He found a copy in the National Library of Australia and arranged to send it to me.

In the end, I would be remiss if I did not recognise the support extended by Palgrave Macmillan, especially Laura Pacey, Joseph Johnson and Rachel Sangster. My wife, Dr Nadia Tahir, Managing Director, Quality Assurance Agency of the Higher Education Commission of Pakistan, made every effort to ensure that I do not compromise on quality. Nevertheless, any failing that remains is exclusively my own and has nothing whatsoever to do with any name mentioned here.

Lahore, Pakistan Pervez Tahir

Note

1. Pervez Tahir, G. C. Harcourt and Prue Kerr, 'On Joan Robinson and China', Ch. 13 of *Joan Robinson. Critical Assessments of Leading Economists*, Vol. 5, edited by Prue Kerr with the collaboration of G. C. Harcourt (London, Routledge, 2002), pp. 267–80.

Acknowledgements (1990)

John Sender and John Toye suggested the idea of writing this volume as part of my doctoral dissertation at Cambridge University, which was completed under the able supervision of Geoff Harcourt. Many of the arguments were drastically recast in the light of Peter Nolan's comments on an earlier draft. I also benefited from the advice of the late Sukhamoy Chakravarty and Lord Kahn. Ajit Singh, Ronald Berger, Sol Adler, Carl Riskin and Liu Minquan were helpful in various ways. The unpublished material is quoted here with the kind permission of the trustees of JVR Collection at King's College. The work on the present version was supported by the award of Joan Robinson Memorial Lectureship in Economics at Cambridge University. Although my debts are enormous, I remain solely responsible for the views and any errors.

Contents

Abbreviations

ACEI	Anglo-Chinese Educational Institute
BCFA	British-China Friendship Association
BCPI	British Council for the Promotion of International Trade
CCPIT	China Committee or the Promotion of International Trade
CPSG	China Policy Study Group
FCFA	Franco-Chinese Friendship Association
JR	Joan Robinson
JVRC	Joan Violet Robinson Collection
NCP	National Conference on Planning
NEP	New Economic Policy
SACU	Society for Anglo-Chinese Understanding
USSR	Union of Soviet Socialist Republics

1

Introduction

Joan Robinson's views of Maoist China do not make sense to many in the economics profession. Some find these "scandalous" (Turner, 1989, 170), others "completely uncritical", even "totally unreliable".[1] She paid eight visits to China—in 1953, 1957, 1963, 1964, 1967, 1972, 1975 and, finally, 1978.[2] The whole experience is seen to be "reminiscent of the Webbs' late love affair with the Soviet Union".[3] If a sympathetic Samuelson is puzzled as to how an independent mind like hers "waxed successively enthusiastic about Stalin's Soviet Union; Mao's China; North Korea; Castro's Cuba; American students' new leftism" (Feiwel, 1989, 862), a friendly Harcourt (1982, 319) has to admit that her "writing in this area contains a deliberate leaven of advocacy". Development economists are sharply critical, too. Streeten believes that "she was wrong about Mao" (Feiwel, *ibid.*). In an interview with the author, Chakravarty stated that Joan Robinson's interest in, and writings on, China were a less interesting aspect of her contributions. Economists with a specialist interest in the development of China hold a similar view. According to Riskin, "her writing about China was probably the least interesting aspect of her work, except in that it revealed views and attitudes that might throw light on

P. Tahir, *Making Sense of Joan Robinson on China*, Palgrave Studies in the History of Economic Thought, https://doi.org/10.1007/978-3-030-28825-9_1

her other concerns". But he hastened to add that "being Joan Robinson, she could not write about anything completely without insight".[4]

It might be said in Joan Robinson's defence that the leaven of advocacy was a way of countering the propaganda of those whose own writings contained a bias in favour of capitalism (Harcourt, 1982, 359). It might also be said that she was not alone in looking at the Chinese experience as a successful strategy of development.[5] A convenient approach would be to dismiss her writings as traveller's tales, which are not expected to contain serious analysis anyway. None of these courses is adopted here. China was isolated and quite misrepresented as well. Who would know better than Joan Robinson that there is no substitute for information and analysis? Even those extremely critical of her other works do not deny her acute analytical prowess. She was thus not expected to respond to propaganda in kind. Further, it is a fact that she shared the illusions about Maoist China with many others. That does not render her position less vulnerable than it is. Further still, her explorations in China and its development were by no means a sideline activity. Some of her main works discuss China as an economy where development was *actually* taking place (Robinson, 1962b, 1968h, 1970g, 1979b; Robinson and Eatwell, 1973).

The main objective of this volume is to focus on the insights by separating analysis from advocacy. Joan Robinson's influence in the developing world exceeded the extent of her serious contribution to development economics. At a time when theories and models of development are being subjected to intense re-examination in view of the accumulation of a considerable fund of experience in the developing countries as well as the availability of more reliable information about socialist economies, it is instructive to look afresh at the insights as well as prejudices acquired by a theorist of the stature of Joan Robinson.

Joan Robinson had "no special knowledge of Chinese history and none at all of the language" (Robinson, 1977b, 7). It is obvious that a writer in her situation is dependent upon interpreters. Observation makes up for the inability to communicate directly only to the extent that the sample being observed is fairly representative of the population. She did not write anything on China in the scholarly economic journals, except for some book reviews. Most of the writings appeared in journals of politics and social issues. Many of them were described variously as "reminiscences", "letters", "notes", "conversations", "reports" and so forth. While Joan

Robinson's China connection has been severely attacked by the right as well as the left,[6] no attempt has been made even to write up her work in a thorough and informative way. This volume is an attempt to do so.

Chapter 2 sets out the main contributions which Joan Robinson made in her work on China. The material—which is enormous, some of it unpublished and most of what is published is in periodicals ranging from the well known to the hardly known or in the form of pamphlets—is organised with a view to getting a grip on the main economic arguments. It is possible to look at her work in three broad phases. The first phase comprises her thinking and writing before the third visit in 1963. As is shown in Chap. 3, despite tremendous enthusiasm for the Chinese experiment, she had her own set of views on how China should develop as a socialist economy. The two field trips served the purpose of gathering some evidence in support of her views. The study of China appears to have provided for Joan Robinson, at least until her third visit or during what is called here the first phase, a laboratory to intuitively test her own thinking about economic development in the backward overpopulated economies. Her ideas in this first phase were broadly similar to the views of the right in China—a high rate of capital accumulation, achieved without an intolerable sacrifice of consumption, profit-oriented industrial management to avoid bureaucratic tendency, use of prices with moral supplements, population control, reward by work done and the extraction of agricultural surplus through gradual collectivisation. Inequality, according to her, is associated with private property. With its elimination, she assumes the prevalence of justice in the nonagriculture sector, though the tax-free collective property differentials in agriculture are seen to be a source of inequality. On the whole, she finds the planning arrangement in China to be working well in industry, but still feels uneasy about the suitability of socialism as a system for agriculture due mainly to the difficulties of organising labour on a large scale.

In the second phase, she takes a sharp turn to the left. Between the Great Leap Forward and the cultural revolution, a period of statistical and informational blackout, she argues that the problems of socialist organisation lie in industry not agriculture. The communes are considered to have resolved the dilemma of organising labour in agriculture, whereas Soviet-type industrial management (even in its reformed decentralised form) is criticised for its profit motivation and a hierarchical structure resulting from differentials caused by intellectual property—an unfortunate outcome of equal-opportunity education. Thus the planning system is plagued not only by its inherent bureaucracy, but also by the inequity of the property system. In the cultural revolution she perceives the possibility of a cooperative system, based on the serve-the-people ideology. Chapter 4 discusses the second phase of her writings, which began after the trip to China in 1963 and lasted until 1975. During this most important phase, enthusiasm for the Chinese experiment turned into advocacy of the Maoist position on economic as well as political issues. Believing as she did in information supplied to her at the time of a statistical blackout, the analysis was constrained by the quality of the information used. It is argued that her incisiveness returns whenever she rids herself of the distorting influence of the prepared information.

It was not until after the death of Mao that she discovered to her horror that the Chinese had not been telling the truth even to trusting analysts. This was the beginning of the third and final phase, which is the subject matter of Chap. 5. With more information available in the post-Mao China, she was able to look back at her previous writings and put some of the record straight. This is a phase of self-criticism, in which Joan Robinson admits to having been starry-eyed about the cultural revolution decade and returns to supporting rightist economic reform. This is not to say that her story is always plausible whenever she is not misled by the Chinese. In some important cases, she does not follow up the logic of her own argument.

The last chapter presents the conclusions of the volume. In the main, it is argued that what is possible to salvage out of her thinking and enthusiasm about the economic development of China is a set of ideas not very different from the views of those dubbed as the rightists in the so-called two-line struggle in Mao's China.

Notes

1. See Chipman's reminiscences and Ilahn's interview in Feiwel (1989, 868, 907).
2. In Robinson (1977b), the note introducing her mentions, incorrectly, only six visits until 1977.

3. Matthews in Feiwel (1989, 912).
4. Carl Riskin's letters to the author, 27 February (1987).
5. See, inter alia, Beitelheim (1958, 1974), Raj (1956) and Reynolds (1975) from across the ideological spectrum. See also India (1956) and Pakistan (1975) for reports by two official delegations of planners from developing countries.
6. For a bitter attack from the radical left, see Robinson (1968d).

References

Unpublished Material

Carl Riskin's letter to the author, 27 February, 1987.

Published Works

Beitelheim, C. (1958) 'China's Economic Growth,' *Economic Weekly*, 10, 1460–4.

———. (1974) *Cultural Revolution and Industrial Organisation in China*. New York: Monthly Review Press.

Feiwel, G.R. (ed.). (1989) *Joan Robinson and Modern Economic Theory*. London: Macmillan.

Government of India. (1956) *Report of the Indian Delegation to China on Agricultural Planning and Techniques*. New Delhi: Government of India Press.

Government of Pakistan (1975) *Economic and Manpower Planning in People's Republic of China: Report of the Delegation of Development Planners and Manpower Experts to People's Republic of China*. Islamabad: Printing Corporation of Pakistan.

Harcourt, G.C. (1982) *The Social Science Imperialists*, P. Kerr (ed.). London: Routledge and Kegan Paul.

Raj, K.N. (1956) 'The Indian and Chinese Plans,' *Economic Weekly*, 8, 699–702.

Reynolds, L.G. (1975) 'China as a Less Developed Economy,' *American Economic Review*, 65(3), 418–28.

Robinson, Joan. (1962b) 'Review of E.S. Kirby (ed.),' *Contemporary China. Economic Journal*, 72, 734.

———. (1968d) 'Reply to Sussex Internationalists' Attack, *SACU News*, 3, 5.

———. (1968h) 'The Decentralised Society. Review of A. Donnithorne,' *China's Economic System, SACU News*, 5.
———. (1970g) *Freedom and Necessity*. London: George Allen and Unwin.
———. (1977b) *Reports from China, 1953–76*. London: Anglo-Chinese Educational Institute.
———. (1979b) *Aspects of Development and Underdevelopment*. Cambridge: Cambridge University Press.
Robinson, Joan and J. Eatwell. (1973) *An Introduction to Modern Economics*. London: McGraw-Hill.
Turner, M.S. (1989) *Joan Robinson and the Americans*. Armonk, NY: M.E. Sharpe.

2

The Contributions

Most of the visits paid by Joan Robinson to China coincided with crucial phases in the Chinese development. At the end of a visit, she would generally bring out publications containing her thoughts and fresh material. This survey is organised around them. While these publications constitute her main contributions, the writings between the visits—articles, reviews, comments, letters and so on—were largely in the nature of further elaborations, clarifications and reactions to criticisms of the main contributions. Joan Robinson had a tendency to reproduce partly or wholly her previous writings on later occasions, sometimes under different titles. In this chapter, an attempt is made to sort out this "double-counting".

Letters from a Visitor to China (1954)

In the summer of 1953 (June–July),[1] Joan Robinson paid her first visit to China. The first phase of the Chinese development, 1949–52, had ended. During this phase, the People's Republic had been engaged in making its revolutionary impact felt through institutional reform, together with the

P. Tahir, *Making Sense of Joan Robinson on China*, Palgrave Studies in the History of Economic Thought, https://doi.org/10.1007/978-3-030-28825-9_2

more immediate task of rehabilitating the war-torn economy. Being in China in 1953, therefore, afforded Joan Robinson an opportunity to analyse the Chinese performance for the outside world. She recorded her first impressions in the form of letters, originally serialised in the *Monthly Review* during 1953–54 and subsequently collected in Robinson (1954a) under the title of *Letters from a Visitor to China*.[2] In addition, in a shorter paper she made a forceful plea to end China's isolation: she pleaded that "Napoleon's sleeping giant had awakened, and there was no use denying either that the giant was a giant or that he was awake" (Robinson, 1954b, 125). In writing the *Letters*, she joined a noted group of authors—Edgar Snow and Han Su-Yin among them—who visited China to tell the world about developments taking place there and, on the international arena dominated by the US-led policy to isolate China, present the Chinese side of the story. The story is told passionately but not uncritically. Yet the questions that are raised cannot but be described as those by a sympathetic critic.

Joan Robinson was impressed by "the clean-and-honest" face of "New China". She considered cleanliness and honesty as important facts to be explained as a visible reflection of "the state of mind" of the Chinese people whereby they asked themselves in wonderment: "How is it that we can perform miracles?" The economic topics briefly touched upon included land reform, industrial and commercial reforms, organisation of trade, technology and manpower, population, basic needs such as food and health and education, management of inflation and the chaotic economic conditions and the economic rights of national minorities.

China: An Economic Perspective (1958)

The second visit took place in the autumn of 1957.[3] While the first visit culminated in her giving out to the world the first impressions of an enthusiast—the *Letters*—the second visit provided a chance for more professional study. The first five-year plan had concluded and the draft of the second five-year plan was under discussion. There is some confusion here, created by Joan Robinson's later remarks that the report based on the second visit was not traceable, despite being published. The reminiscences she provided instead say nothing about the developments taking place in the Chinese economy (Robinson, 1977b, 7, 37–9). Berger thinks that the missing report was published by the Britain-China Friendship Association (BCFA), from which those sympathetic to the Chinese line in the Sino-Soviet conflict had broken off to form the Society for Anglo-Chinese Understanding (SACU).[4] However, a search of the relevant records did not confirm the existence of the report, published or unpublished. Sol Adler, who was with Joan Robinson during the visit in question, recollected that she had written something in 1957 for the American periodical *Nation*.[5] Robinson (1957a, b) were published in it, but before the visit to China. Their subjects were Baran and Sweezy, not China directly. In 1958, the British periodical *New Statesman and Nation* did carry a piece on the specific subject of the Chinese attitude towards birth control (Robinson, 1958a), but nothing in the nature of a general economic report. Her own personal records do not provide any clue either.[6]

Most probably, the report in question was prepared but not published separately. It formed part of Robinson and Adler (1958), a Fabian tract under the professional sounding title—*China: An Economic Perspective.*[7] The non-availability of the 1957 report does not cause a serious gap as the *Economic Perspective* and the article on birth control (Robinson, 1958a) together throw enough light on her sojourn in China in 1957. Robinson and Adler (1958) is among the earliest attempts to formulate a proper economic perspective of the Chinese economy for the Western world in terms the latter would understand. The contribution deals with the rate of development, estimation of national income, the state of the Chinese statistics, living standards, wage differentials, the spread of cooperatives in agriculture, the factory system and the problem of overpopulation. Although *Economic Perspective* was published after the Great Leap had been launched, it "deliberately refrained" from discussing the developments since the visit in 1957, so as to look at the long-term prospects of industrial development in China, with the main role of agriculture being to provide a surplus for industrial investment.

The understanding of Joan Robinson's perspective on the Chinese economy is significantly aided by contributions that have not been published. In 1957 she delivered the following lectures in China[8]:

1. The relations between the rate of accumulation and the price level.
2. The problem of the choice of techniques for a planned economy in the way which China is developing—that is to say, with limited industrial resources.
3. How far and in what way the price system can be useful in a planned economy.

Notes from China (1964)

Her well-known interest in agricultural communes and the strategy of "walking on two legs" began after the third visit in the summer of 1963. Until this visit, Joan Robinson did not make any significant contribution. She reviewed two books on China (Robinson, 1960d, 1962b). During this interval, the Russians had pulled out, China had embarked upon the Leap, the cooperatives were very rapidly converted into communes and the now-known famine had occurred. Some issues arising out of these developments were briefly touched on in Robinson and Berger (1961, 222). In the beginning, Joan Robinson expressed greater keenness about the urban rather than the agricultural communes. During the visit, a press interview was published.[9] Soon after the visit in 1963, a short piece appeared in an Indian periodical on the Chinese view (Robinson, 1963c).

It was only in the following year that in a flurry of writings, she explained and advocated the concept of the commune as a bold new initiative for agrarian advance and transformation. The radical measures taken during the Leap had by this time been in operation for some time, making it possible to attempt at least a preliminary evaluation. The contributions include Robinson (1964a, b, c, d, e). By far the best analysis was presented in Robinson (1964d), which was reproduced with minor changes as Robinson (1966c, d) and in full as Robinson (1973c).[10] Robinson (1964e) was reprinted as Robinson (1965b). The booklet, *Notes from China* (Robinson 1964h),[11] reproduces Robinson (1964c) as it is and Robinson (1964f) with minor alterations. As the Soviet Union, following the ideological rift with China, started to criticise China in the world on top of the US efforts to isolate it, Joan Robinson also took on the job of explaining "The Chinese Point of View", which is the exact title of Robinson (1964f). Further, she made an attempt to assess the prospects for China in a 20-year perspective in Robinson (1964g), which is too short and is judgemental rather than an empirical study. In October 1964, Joan Robinson paid her fourth and the shortest visit to China, informing the world about "What's New in China" in Robinson (1965c). The effort was nothing more than hurriedly formed impressions, while she waited in Beijing to make her first trip to North Korea.[12]

The interval between the fourth and the fifth visit seems to be a period of study and reflection, with some 15 books on various aspects of Chinese economy and society reviewed by Joan Robinson.[13] Robinson (1965g) was slightly edited and reproduced as Robinson (1966f) in the context of the debate on socialist economic reform. Liberman's reform was adopted in the Soviet Union with effect from September 1969. It was denounced as "revisionistic" by the Chinese. With Joan Robinson also among those who looked at the cultural revolution as the Chinese response to Soviet reform, her contributions to the debate on socialist economic reform, Robinson (1965h, 1967g, h), provided an important backdrop to her own first-hand account of the cultural revolution. In this context, her short intervention in the debate on the modelling of producer cooperatives is also significant (Robinson, 1967b).

The Cultural Revolution in China (1969)

In November 1967, Joan Robinson visited China for the fifth time. This visit exclusively focused on comprehending the cultural revolution. She gave her immediate reactions in December in an Indian periodical (Robinson, 1967i) and in February 1968 in the newsletter of the SACU (Robinson, 1968b), which she had to defend against a bitter onslaught from a group of British radicals (Robinson, 1968d). Her considered view of the cultural revolution, presented first in the oft-quoted article Robinson (1968c) and in the subsequent year in the well-known book *The Cultural Revolution in China* (Robinson, 1969a),[14] was no different from her initial reactions. Actually this book substantially contains the three contributions preceding it (Robinson, 1967i, 1968b, c). As the preface of the book was written in April 1968, which is also the date of publication of Robinson (1968c), it seems that the three articles were written as parts of the first chapter of the book. Joan Robinson herself mentions the use of Robinson (1967i, 1968c) in the preface. Robinson (1968b), which is used by Joan Robinson more than the other two but without acknowledging the fact, is not a very well-known contribution. The rest of the book chronicles the important events of the cultural revolution and reproduces a number of significant documents. As she put it, these "give far more insight into what was involved than can any analysis by an external observer" (Robinson, 1969a, preface). A postscript, written in 1968, also forms part of the book.

Robinson (1970a) gives her reaction to a review of *The Cultural Revolution*. Until the sixth visit to China in 1972, her writings on China show a marked influence of the cultural revolution. She became ever more confident and assertive about the Chinese economic future. This is borne out, on the one hand, by her reviews of the two Myrdal's and, on the other, the lectures delivered by her on the Chinese economic policy. Robinson (1968a, 1971b) reviews two of Jan Myrdal's contributions on China. Gunnar Myrdal's *Asian Drama* is reviewed in Robinson (1968f), and the conclusion is drawn that the failure of the South Asian economies such as India and Pakistan to deal with basic economic problems is the consequence of what Myrdal describes as the "soft states". In another review of the same book, China is portrayed as having solved these problems because the Chinese "state is anything but soft" (Robinson, 1968h, 383).[15] Robinson (1969d) also concentrates on proving the superiority of Chinese socialism over the Indian variety. Robinson (1968e) is a lecture delivered at the Royal Society of Arts and Robinson (1970c) is a paper read at a conference on China. Both analyse the development of the Chinese economy since liberation in 1949. Robinson (1970d, e, 1971a) are reproductions of a lecture given in 1969 on the bases of "Chinese Economic Policy" in Mao's "ten great relationships".[16] Mao's view of history as "continuous development from the realm of necessity to the realm of freedom" was explored in *Freedom and Necessity*; a separate chapter on China suggested that, compared with the capitalist and other socialist economies, it had found a way to marry freedom and necessity in a humane framework (Robinson, 1970g, 100–4).

Among the other writings on China before her visit in 1972 are included two book reviews, Robinson (1968h, 1970b); two introductions to books on China, Robinson (1969e, 1970f); one short comment to mark the first ten years of the communes, Robinson (1969b); a short note and a letter to project China's foreign policy moves (Robinson, 1968g; Needham and Robinson, 1969[17]) and a letter focusing on the difficulties of the Great Leap and the analogous situation in the Soviet development (Robinson, 1969f).

Economic Management in China, 1972 (1973)

By the time Joan Robinson returned to China in April 1972 for her sixth visit spread over six weeks, the economic and political climate seemed to her to be in a settled enough state to talk about economic management. The booklet *Economic Management in China, 1972* (Robinson, 1973f) is the main contribution of this period.[18] Robinson (1972a, 1973d) form the first two sections of Robinson (1973f). Robinson (1973e) is also based on the material from *Economic Management*, the foreword of which describes it as an "account of the system of planning and management which is evolving in China in the 'period of transformation' emerging from 'the struggle and criticism' of the cultural revolution". *Economic Management* ran into a second edition in which were added a postscript and a few minor points of detail that took note of the events since her visit in 1972 (Robinson, 1975c).[19] Robinson (1972b), which reviews three books on China, indicates her exasperation with the manner in which information was managed in the Lin Piao affair.

While her interest in socialist economic reform had continued (Robinson, 1973g), the year 1974 provided an opportunity to look back at the achievements of a generation, as the People's Republic had come into being in 1949 (Robinson, 1974c), as well as an occasion to compare the Chinese revolution with the Russian revolution (Robinson, 1974d). Robinson (1975d), which is a foreword to a pamphlet on the Chinese education, and Robinson (1975e), a book review in the journal *History*, were written in the hilarious mood of what she thought were the successes of the cultural revolution. In August 1974, while introducing the second edition of the third volume of her *Collected Economic Papers*, she stated with some satisfaction: "My traveller's tales from Asia [1965] were first greeted with scepticism, but recently many observers have confirmed them and I am now quite in the fashion" (Robinson, 1975b, xiv).

Reports from China, 1953–1976 (1977)

Joan Robinson embarked on her seventh visit to China in May 1975 to study the Chinese method of dealing with the tricky question of the economic and social development of the peoples and regions falling outside the mainstream. Robinson (1975f, g, h) are concerned with this aspect of her contributions. Robinson (1975f) is also reproduced in Robinson (1977b, 121–31). She admitted that the "story of Tibet or of Sinkiang is more dramatic and more important", but she never really analysed their problems.[20] Her visit was confined to Hsishuang-panna autonomous prefecture in the province of Yunnan. The visit "provided a glimpse of a fascinating scene that could well repay years of study" (Robinson, 1975f, 32). All the same she feared accusations of having "just made it all up" (Robinson, 1975g, 23).

She is clearly perturbed over the Lin Piao affair in Robinson (1975i). Though still critical of China-watchers' view of China (Robinson, 1976a, 92), Joan Robinson had begun to ask questions about the cultural revolution (Robinson, 1976b, 51).[21] With the benefit of hindsight, a selection of the past writings was put together as *Reports from China, 1953–1976* (Robinson, 1977b).[22]

China Since Mao

Mao died in September 1976. But Joan Robinson took some time to collect her thoughts after Mao. In May 1978, she made her eighth and the last trip to China. She did not write directly about her experience this time. However, when Beitelheim (1978b) dubbed the post-Mao reform as "the great leap backward", she wrote a strong rebuttal (Robinson, 1978c). It was reprinted (Robinson, 1979e) by the *Monthly Review* (May

1979, 2) "to clarify the anti-Bettelheim view" in its coverage of the debate on China since Mao. In the following year, Joan Robinson returned to this debate in Robinson (1979f), appropriately titled "the pros and cons". Coincidentally, the Western translation of Mao's critique of Soviet economics was published after his death (Mao Tse-tung, 1977a, b). The two reviews of it by Joan Robinson, as also the review of the second edition of a book containing material written before 1976, again reflect her approach to the questions raised in the debate on China since Mao (Robinson, 1978d, 1979d, 1980b). Robinson (1982) is her last writing on China.

Notes

1. *The Times*, 13 June 1953.
2. Robinson (1954a) is sometimes referred to in this volume as the *Letters*.
3. *The Times*, 21 August 1957.
4. Interview with Ronald Berger, 20 February (1987). A colleague of Joan Robinson at SACU, he first visited China in 1959 and with her in 1975. See Robinson and Berger (1961) for a BBC discussion between the two.
5. Sol Adler's letter from Beijing, 30 November (1986).
6. JVR Collection, King's Modem Archives. There is something amiss about 1957. Even the passport containing the entry of the visit to China in 1957 is missing! The only writing on China in 1957 is on "The Chinese Classical Theatre" in the Manchester Guardian Weekly of 19 September 1957 under the initials "JR". Robinson (1977b, 7, 38) indicates an interest in the subject.
7. Sometimes this publication is referred to in this volume as *Economic Perspective*.
8. JVR Collection, iii/5.1–5.3. King's College Library, Cambridge.
9. *Survey of China's Mainland Press*, 6 September 1963.
10. Robinson (1973c) was included in the first edition (1973) of the readings collected by Wilber in *The Political Economy of Development and Underdevelopment* but omitted in the second edition (1979), which came out after the death of Mao.
11. Robinson (1964h) has sometimes been referred to in this volume as *Notes* for short.
12. This quick trip became the basis of Robinson (1965d), which described North Korean economy as a miracle. She was not impressed by Cuba

(interview with Berger, 20 February 1987), which she re-visited in 1965. See Robinson (1965e), reproduced as Robinson (1966b).

13. Robinson (1964j, 1965f, g, 1966a, e, f, g, 1967c, d, e, f).
14. Robinson (1969a) is also mentioned in this volume as *The Cultural Revolution* for short.
15. Robinson (1969c) is a reproduction of Robinson (1968h).
16. The lecture was given to the Anglo-Chinese Educational Institute (ACEI) on 21 November 1969.
17. The letter was sent to *The Times* jointly by Joseph Needham and Joan Robinson as chairman and vice chairman of SACU, but it was refused publication.
18. Robinson (1973f) is mentioned in this volume as the *Economic Management* for short.
19. A review note in *Broadsheet* (March 1975, last page) states that Joan Robinson visited China in the summer of 1974. The information seems to be based on the title of the postscript written in 1974 for the second edition of *Economic Management*—"Postscript—summer 1974" (Robinson, 1975c, 42). The fact, however, is that Joan Robinson did not visit China in 1974. The postscript in question was written on the basis of reports from other visitors, particularly Berger (1974) and Daly (1974).
20. Except of course for the brief mention in *Economic Management*: "The autonomous regions have planned revenue which is much less than expenditure. For example, since 1960 the bulk of Tibet's budget has been financed and 30 per cent of its grain supply provided by the central authorities. By this means, the government is taxing the relatively richer part of the population to cover its own outlay and to even up development for the poorest" (Robinson, 1973f, 30).
21. Her fascination with North Korea continued, as is evident from Robinson (1976a, 92, 1977c).
22. Robinson (1977b) is also referred as *Reports* in subsequent discussion in this volume.

References

Unpublished Material

Interview with Ronald Berger, 20 February, 1987.
Sol Adler's letter from Beijing, 30 November, 1986.

Published Works

Beitelheim, C. (1978b) 'The Great Leap Backward,' *Monthly Review*, 30, 37–130.

Berger, R. (1974) 'Chinese Economic Planning,' *Broadsheet*, 11, 1–3.

Daly, P. (1974) 'China 1974: Growth without Waste,' *China Now*, 45, 3–4.

Mao Tse-tung. (1977a) 'On the Cooperative Transformation of Agriculture [1955],' in *Selected Works*, Vol. 5, 184–207, 1955. Peking: Foreign Languages Press.

———. (1977b) *A Critique of Soviet Economics*. New York: Monthly Review Press.

Monthly Review. (1979) 'Editorial,' 31, 1–19.

Needham, J. and Joan Robinson. (1969) 'Too Much for *The Times*,' *SACU News*, 4, 1–2.

Robinson, Joan. (1954a) *Letters from a Visitor to China*. Cambridge: Students' Bookshops.

———. (1954b) 'Britain and China,' *Nation*, 179, 125–8.

———. (1957a) 'The Policy of Backward Nations. Review of BARAN (1957),' *Nation*, 184, 485–6.

———. (1957b) 'Clues to History,' Rejoinder to Paul Sweezy. *Nation*, 185, opp. L.

———. (1958a) 'Birth Control in China,' *New Statesman and Nation*, 55, 66–7.

———. (1960d) 'Review of T.T. Hughes and D.E.T. Luard,' *The Economic Development of Communist China, Economic Journal*, 70, 409–10.

———. (1962b) 'Review of E.S. Kirby (ed.),' *Contemporary China. Economic Journal*, 72, 734.

———. (1963c) 'The Chinese View,' *Seminar*, 50, 44–6.

———. (1964a) 'Communes in China,' *Listener*, 71, 177–89.

———. (1964b) 'Notes from China,' *Economic Weekly*, 16, 195–203.

———. (1964c) 'A British Economist on Chinese Communes,' *Eastern Horizon*, 3, 6–11.

———. (1964d) 'Chinese Agricultural Communes,' *Coexistence*, 1, 1–6.

———. (1964e) 'The Chinese Communes,' *Political Quarterly*, 35, 285–97.

———. (1964f) 'The Chinese Point of View,' *International Affairs*, 40, 232–44.

———. (1964g) 'Prospects for China,' *New Scientist*, 22, 756.

———. (1964h) *Notes from China*. Oxford: Basil Blackwell.

———. (1964j) 'Review of S.H. Chou,' *The Chinese Inflation, 1937–1949, Economic Journal*, 74, 680–1.

———. (1965b) 'China, 1963: The Communes,' in Robinson (1965a), 192–206.
———. (1965c) 'What's New in China?' *Eastern Horizon*, 4, 11–5.
———. (1965d) 'Korean Miracle,' *Monthly Review*, 16 (9), 541–9.
———. (1965e) 'Cuba, 1965,' *Economic Weekly*, 17, 1341–5.
———. (1965f) Review of Ta-chung Liu and Kung-chia Yeh, *The Economy of Chinese Mainland: National Income and Economic Development, 1933–1959. Economic Journal*, 75, 604.
———. (1965g) 'Economic Principles in China,' Review of C. Bettelheim, et al., *Construction du Socialisme en Chine, Broadsheet*, 2, 1–3.
———. (1965h) Review of P.J.D. Wiles, *The Political Economy of Communism*, in Robinson, (1965a), 82–91.
———. (1966a) 'Review of Walker (1965),' *International Affairs*, 42, 159–60.
———. (1966b) 'Cuba—1965,' *Monthly Review*, 17, 10–18.
———. (1966c) 'China Today: The Organisation of Agriculture,' *Bulletin of the Atomic Scientists*, 22, 28–32.
———. (1966d) 'Organisation of Agriculture,' in R. Adams (ed.), *Contemporary China*. London: Peter Owen.
———. (1966e) 'Reviews of Chen Chi-yi, *La Reforme Agraire en Chine Populaire;* Yuan-li Wu. *The Steel Industry In Communist China,' International Affairs*, July 42, 546–8.
———. (1966f) 'Review of C. Bettelheim, et al., La Construction du Socialisme en Chine,' *Coexistence*, 3, 105–7.
———. (1966g) 'The Communes and the Great Leap Forward,' Reviews of Crook and Crook (1965); Dumont (1966). *New Left Review*, 37, 69–72.
———. (1967b) 'The Soviet Collective Farm as a Producer Cooperative: Comment,' *American Economic Review*, 57(1), 222–3.
———. (1967c) 'Reviews of Yuan-li Wu, *The Economy of Communist China*, D.H. Perkins *Market Control and Planning in Communist China*; J.L. Buck, L. Dawson and Yuan-li Wu, *Food and Agriculture in Communist China.' International Affairs*, 43, 192–3.
———. (1967d) 'Reviews of A.N. Young, *China's Wartime Finance and Inflation, 1937–1945, and Foreign Investment*; Chi-ming Hou, *Economic Development in China, 1840–1937,' International Affairs*, 43, 404–6.
———. (1967e) 'Review of H. P. Ortisch,' *Eyewitness in China, International Affairs*, 43, 611–2.
———. (1967f) 'Review of *The Awakening of China, 1793–1949,' International Affairs*, 43, 797.

———. (1967g) 'The Economic Reforms,' *Monthly Review*, 19, 45–50.
———. (1967h) 'Socialist Affluence,' in C.H. Feinstein (ed.), *Socialism, Capitalism and Economic Growth: Essays in Honour of Maurice Dobb*. London: Cambridge University Press. Also in Robinson, (1973a), 33–47.
———. (1967i) 'The Chinese Cultural Revolution,' *Now*, 22 December.
———. (1968a) 'Review of Jan Myrdal,' *Report from a Chinese Village, International Affairs*, 44, 152–3.
———. (1968b) 'Intensive Look at China,' *SACU News*, 3, 1–5.
———. (1968c) 'The Cultural Revolution in China,' *International Affairs*, 44, 214–27.
———. (1968d) 'Reply to Sussex Internationalists' Attack, *SACU News*, 3, 5.
———. (1968e) 'China Today: Economic Organisation,' *Journal of the Royal Society of Arts*, 116, 683–93.
———. (1968f) 'The Poverty of Nations. Review of Myrdal (1968),' *Listener*, 80, 509–10, 517.
———. (1968g) 'One Quarter of Mankind,' *Canadian Forum*, 48, 150. 'Review of Myrdal,' *Cambridge Quarterly*, 3, 381–9.
———. (1968h) 'The Decentralised Society. Review of A. Donnithorne,' *China's Economic System, SACU News*, 5.
———. (1969a) *The Cultural Revolution in China*. Harmondsworth, Middlesex: Penguin Books.
———. (1969b) 'Ten Years of Communes,' *Broadsheet*, 6, 3.
———. (1969c) 'Review of Myrdal (1968),' *Canadian Dimension*, 5, 27–30.
———. (1969d) 'India and China: A Comparison,' *Listener*, 82, 816–18.
———. (1969e) 'Preface,' in N. Brunner (ed.), *China's Economy*. London: Anglo-Chinese Educational Institute, 1–2.
———. (1969f) Letter to *Tribune*, 24 January.
———. (1970a) 'Reply to A.J. Watson,' *China Now*, 2, 4.
———. (1970b) Reviews of K. Buchanan, *The Transformation of the Chinese Earth*; T.R. Tregear, *Economic Geography of China, Broadsheet*, 7, last page.
———. (1970c) 'Society and Economics in China Today,' in R. Jungk, et al., *China and the West: Mankind Evolving*. London: Granstone Press, 35–47.
———. (1970d) 'Chinese Economic Policy,' *Studium Generale*, 23, 1267–74.
———. (1970e) 'Chinese Economic Policy: Prescription for Development,' *China Now*, 4, 5–8.
———. (1970f) 'Foreword,' in E.L. Wheelwright and B. McFarlane (eds.), *The Chinese Road to Socialism*. New York: Monthly Review Press.
———. (1970g) *Freedom and Necessity*. London: George Allen and Unwin.

———. (1971a) 'Chinese Economic Policy,' in J. Needham, et al., *Hand and Brain in China and Other Essays*. London: Anglo-Chinese Educational Institute, 19–27.

———. (1971b) 'Something to Live for. Review of J. Myrdal and G. Kessle,' *The Revolution Continued New Statesman*, 81, 631–3.

———. (1972a) 'For Use, Not for Profit,' *Eastern Horizon*, 1l, 6–15.

———. (1972b) 'Through Western Spectacles,' Reviews of K. Mehnert, *China Today*; Terrill (1972); and K. Ling, *Red Guard, Spectator*, 7522, 321.

———. (1973c) 'Chinese Agricultural Communes,' in C.K. Wilber (ed.) (1973). *The Political Economy of Development and Underdevelopment*. New York: Random House, 209–15.

———. (1973d) 'Structure of Management,' *China Now*, 29, 10–11.

———. (1973e) 'Planning and Management in China Today,' *Cambridge Review*, 94, 106–20.

———. (1973f) *Economic Management in China, 1972*. London: Anglo-Chinese Educational Institute.

———. (1973g) 'Review of W. Brus,' *The Market in a Socialist Economy, Economic Journal*, 83, 258–60.

———. (1974c) 'Achievements of a Generation,' *China Now*, 45, 2–3.

———. (1974d) 'Two Revolutions,' *Broadsheet*, 11, 4.

———. (1975b) 'Introduction 1974: Comments and Explanations,' in *Collected Economic Papers*, Vol. 3, 2nd ed. Oxford: Basil Blackwell, iii–xiv.

———. (1975c) *Economic Management in China*. 2nd ed. London: Anglo-Chinese Educational Institute.

———. (1975d) 'Foreword,' in P. Mauger et al., *Education in China*. London: Anglo-Chinese Educational Institute, 1–2.

———. (1975e) Review of Leslie R. Marchant,' *To Phoenix Seat: An Introductory Study of Maoism and the Chinese Communist Quest for a Paradise on Earth, History*, 60, 272–3.

———. (1975f) 'National Minorities in Yunnan,' *Eastern Horizon*, 14, 32–43.

———. (1975g) 'In the Deep Southwest,' *New China Magazine*, 1, 721–3.

———. (1975h) 'Hsishuang Parma,' *China Now*, 55, 10–11, 15–16.

———. (1975i) 'The Fall of Lin Piao.' Review of P. Worsley, *Inside China*; K.S. Karol, *The Second Chinese Evolution, Spectator*, 7677, 217.

———. (1976a) 'Review of J.K. Fairbank, et al.,' *East Asia: Tradition and Transformation, Journal of Royal Asiatic Society* 76, 91–2.

———. (1976b) 'An Eyewitness Account of the Cultural Revolution,' Review of John and Elsie Collier, *China's Socialist Revolution, Monthly Review*, 28, 50–1.

———. (1977b) *Reports from China, 1953–76.* London: Anglo-Chinese Educational Institute.
———. (1977c) 'Review of E. Brun and J. Hersh. *Socialist Korea: A Case Study in the Strategy of Economic Development,*' *Monthly Review* 29, 60–2.
———. (1978c) 'China 1978: Comments on Bettelheim,' *China Now*, 80, 4–7.
———. (1978d) 'Review of Mao Tse-tung (1977),' *China Now*, 80, 26–7.
———. (1979d) 'Review of MAO (1977),' *Monthly Review*, 30, 52–3.
———. (1979e) 'China since Mao,' *Monthly Review*, 31, 48–56.
———. (1979f) 'The Pros and Cons,' *China Now*, 86, 25–6.
———. (1980b) Review of N. Maxwell (ed.) *China's Road to Development, Broadsheet*, 17, last page.
———. (1982) 'Introduction,' *China Now*, 100, 3.
Robinson, Joan and S. Adler. (1958) *China: An Economic Perspective*. London: Fabian International Bureau, Fabian Tract No. 314.
Robinson, Joan and R. Berger. (1961) 'Thinking about China: The Economic Impact of Communism,' *Listener*, 2 February 1961, 65, 220–2.
Wilber, C.K. (ed.) (1973) *The Political Economy of Development and Underdevelopment*. New York: Random House. Also 2nd ed. 1979.

3

The First Phase: Thoughts on Socialist Development in a Backward Overpopulated Economy

The first phase covers the writings of Joan Robinson based on the first two visits to China and the news from China until her third visit in 1963. First, it is shown that before visiting China in 1953, Joan Robinson had a set of views on socialist development and how China might differ from the Soviet strategy of development. It will then be seen that while the actual contact with China fills her with enthusiasm, it does not significantly modify the development scenario assumed by her for a backward overpopulated economy.

The Views Set from the Beginning

Before visiting China, Joan Robinson's thinking was characterised by three important economic notions. First, the rise of socialism and economic backwardness were intimately linked. Six years before the Chinese revolution and a decade before her first visit to that country, Joan Robinson, in her review of Schumpeter (1943), had emphatically stated that the rise of socialism in the backward Soviet Union rather than a developed capitalist economy of the West was not a fluke, but a path to

P. Tahir, *Making Sense of Joan Robinson on China*, Palgrave Studies in the History of Economic Thought, https://doi.org/10.1007/978-3-030-28825-9_3

development no less important than "the more subtle process of evolution according to the imminent characteristics of capitalism" (Robinson, 1943a, 383). Just before the setting up of a socialist state in China, she felt more confident to declare that the view that socialism would supersede capitalism was nothing more than a dogma. But it was "a proven fact that the Soviet system shows how technical achievements of capitalism can be imitated (in some spheres surpassed)" by backward countries (Robinson, 1949, 64).[1] Second, the resource-rich Soviet Union could afford to neglect population policy; the overpopulated economies would need one. The very first direct reference to China was in the context of its known demographic problem, and what she thought to be the attitude of Marxist theorists to the population question. She maintained:

> Because Malthus was a sanctimonious reactionary, and because Russia had huge reserves of untapped natural resources, Marxists have always brushed overpopulation aside as a capitalist bogey. Now that, it seems, communism is about to be established in a Malthusian nation, the future course of history will be strongly influenced by the philosophy of population which Marxism evolves. (Robinson, 1949, 64)

Third, the Soviet Union had not succeeded in instituting a planning and management system that would avoid the domination of consumers by producers. From the first, Joan Robinson believed that both capitalism and the Soviet system promoted producer's initiative rather than consumer's sovereignty (Robinson, 1949, 61–2). She had also been perturbed about the problem of excess demand in the Soviet economy (Robinson, 1952a, 57).

She stood by the aforementioned economic notions after her first encounter with the Chinese situation, despite the fact that the authorities there took a different view of population. In the *Letters*, she asserted that China furnished the final proof about socialism as a substitute for capitalist development. The Chinese were free

> from the mental contortions of trying to apply Marxism out of the book to their problems. Marx thought of communism as arising out of the explosion of capitalism at its most developed point. China seems to provide the

final proof that Communism is not a stage beyond capitalism but a substitute for it. (Robinson, 1954a, 8)

China enjoyed the great advantage that it did not have to bear "the penalty of being first" in socialist industrialisation. China's "vast experiment in modernization" led Joan Robinson to predict that its industrialisation would be historically as important "in the second half of the twentieth century as that of America in the second half" of the earlier century. She suggested that "the Chinese with their innate sense of form in thought and action have a better chance than any other nation to achieve industrialization without the soulless philistinism" that characterised the industrial revolution in the capitalist West (Robinson, 1954b, 125–8).

Joan Robinson felt frustrated over the lack of acceptance for a population policy. She saw China "bubbling over with babies". The first ever census was underway. The Chinese were "speculating as to whether the population will be nearer to 600 million than the traditional figure of 400 million". She expected natural increase to have accelerated "with a bound", as the improved state of health had reduced the death rate, especially infant mortality and maternal deaths, without a corresponding fall in the birth rate (Robinson, 1954a, 30). In spite of the alarming rise in population, the Chinese took an ideological position against a population policy. She wrote:

> No one will hear of Malthus. Birth control is too much associated with a pessimistic, defeatist, anti-Marxist view of life; they say that the cultivable area of China can be doubled ... and yields can be increased on existing land by scientific farming. [She agreed that] "of mere space there is no lack", [but this] meet[sl the Malthusian argument in its crudest form. It does not counter what seems to me the most cogent point, that the standard of life in physical consumption and in culture and amenities can be raised the faster the more investment goes into raising capital per head, as opposed to catering for more heads. (*Ibid.*, 30–1)

She noticed as the main element of "economic discipline" the existence of a network of supply and marketing cooperatives, which helped to achieve stability without "price regulation by decree". The government agencies controlled the agricultural wholesaling entirely. The peasants sold their after-tax surplus to supply and marketing cooperatives, who, in turn, sold it to government corporations. These corporations fixed the prices. The agricultural commodities were sold to public as well as private enterprises. As for manufactures such as cloth, soap and fertilisers, the wholesaling was only partially in the hands of corporations. Urban retailing was predominantly private, but rural retailing was increasingly moving into the hands of supply and marketing cooperatives (*ibid.*). These were the beginnings of a system that was extolled by Joan Robinson in her later writings for promoting the consumer interest rather than the producer initiative.

Leaving the attitude to birth control aside, Marxism to the Chinese "is a matter of learning from the achievements and from the mistakes of Russia and adapting the lessons to Chinese conditions, without any Hegelian metaphysics to cloud the operation of common sense" (Robinson, 1954a, 7–8).[2] The Russians had made their worst mistakes in agriculture. Joan Robinson discussed the role of agriculture in socialist development only after contact with China. During the first visit, she seemed quite happy with the concept of land reform and the pace of implementation. But she viewed them as transitional. Conceptually, land was distributed per head, with landlords allowed to retain "the same share of land as was given to the poor peasants". A land tax of "about 15 per cent of the main crops", levied "on a sliding scale" and "with various allowances", replaced "50 per cent rents". As the "prices of manufactures are still high", agriculture also "contributes to the national economy through the element of tax and state profit in the prices of goods bought". In addition, the rural sector benefited from cheap loans, marketing through the co-ops, the provision of relief in floods and famines, control of rivers and increased access to health and education services (*ibid.*, 27–30).

The economic and social impact of land reform was becoming visible. First, Joan Robinson found that there "has been a big jump in crop yields already, due to better work and investing the surplus formerly paid in rent in fertilizers, insecticides, draft animals and better ploughs". Second, there was some indication of farmers buying incentive goods: "besides clothes and bedding, villagers are buying gumboots, bicycles, fountain pens, watches and thermos flasks". For the peasants, "the organisation of their first co-operative farm ... opened a new world of intellectual interest... calling out talents they had not known that they possessed" (*ibid.*, 28–9). Only a handful of state farms and a few collectives in Manchuria had been set up at that time. The policy was "to use no compulsion but to educate the peasants to want the change", and to move forward through "three stages of development -mutual aid teams formed ad hoc to get in a harvest, permanent teams, and co-operative farms" (*ibid.*, 29). In the village she studied, only 9 per cent of the families had joined hands in a cooperative. The organising principles were as follows:

1. Private ownership of individual holdings
2. Pooling of land and labour for a common crop programme
3. Cooperative ownership of animals, tools and carts (earning supplementary income for the co-op)
4. Product distribution in proportion to land and labour contribution—30 per cent for the former and 70 per cent for the latter
5. Calculation of labour contribution by allotting points according to skill-weighted hours worked
6. Vegetable gardens and geese in private hands, though the cooperative ownership was beginning to enter into vegetables

No matter how successful, land reform was only the first step towards transforming the traditional agriculture. It was "no permanent solution". Joan Robinson gave three reasons. First, there would be the adverse impact of demographic factors. With the passage of time, "births, deaths and marriages will have made family sizes out of line with holdings". Second, the danger of land reform culminating again into an iniquitous structure was there too: "sales of land are permitted (with certain restrictions) so that, left to itself, inequality would emerge again. Third, land reform provided "a break with the feudal past, and the foundation for a socialist future, not a new system in itself". Despite the yield improvements that had been achieved as a result of land reform,

> clearly a thorough-going reorganisation of agriculture will be necessary to increase yields further and to release manpower for industry. The great

> plains seem to cry out for mechanization. Will the peasants be ready to co-operate by the time industry is ready to provide the machinery? (Robinson, 1954a, 28–9)

Collectivisation would be necessary, though she wondered:

> Will the transition to collective farming be made smoothly? That is the great question—the great test of the whole affair. (*Ibid.*)

Another area for the Chinese to avoid the repetition of the Soviet mistakes was the role of private sector in the nonagricultural activities. As with agricultural reform, Joan Robinson had expressed no views on this aspect until her first visit to China.

The impression she formed was one of a slow but steady socialisation

> without a root-and-branch objection to capitalism as such. Private capitalism in all but the key positions of transport and heavy industry is being fostered and encouraged to make a contribution to industrialization, and so is handicraft production, which is still a very important element in the Chinese economy. (Robinson, 1954a, 7)

While railways and heavy industry were nationalised, "quite a large area of pure private enterprise in miscellaneous industry and trade" was allowed side by side. There was also a mixed sector, where the private sector processed raw materials for the public sector on commission. By retaining a role for the private capitalist, Joan Robinson believed that the Chinese provided a major instance of their capacity to learn from the Soviet experience. Comparisons were often drawn between the period of what the Chinese called "New Democracy" (1949–52) and the New Economic Policy (NEP) in the Soviet Union. But to her they differed in an important respect:

> N.E.P. in Russia was a step back from an over-hasty rush towards socialism. The present phase in China is intended to lead smoothly into socialism without wasting any scrap of resources meanwhile. (*Ibid.*)

What is known as the "five-antis" campaign against the vices of private enterprise had "blown over" by the time Joan Robinson arrived. She admitted the harshness of the campaign, "but a man with patience and clear conscience got pretty fair treatment in the end". The purpose, in her view, was openness, not victimisation. Joan Robinson was not alone in suggesting that the campaign against private businessmen was not a programme for their total abolition. Schumpeter (1968, 318), for instance, believed similarly. During the cultural revolution, however, Robinson was told that the "five-antis" campaign was the response of the party to the increasing influence of the rightists. After the first visit and before the second, one notices a deepening faith in her view of socialist development, shorn of the Soviet mistakes. In 1955, she remarked:

> Squeezing the surplus out of an under-nourished peasantry is certainly a daunting prospect. This is the issue over which the socialist economies now admit that they made their worst mistakes (a year or two will show whether China is going to provide an exception). (Robinson, 1956b, 8)

In lectures delivered in Delhi, she was "now clear that the revolutionary transition to socialism does not come in the advanced capitalist nations, but in the most backward". With an obvious reference to China, she re-affirmed her view that "socialism is not a stage beyond capitalism but a substitute for it". It was better suited to ensure rapid accumulation in underdeveloped countries. The socialist alternative was "a means to achieve rapid accumulation under a different set of the rules of the game":

> Under these rules, it would be possible to decide on a higher rate of capital accumulation by taking a general view of the economy rather than leaving it to the capitalists' whims, to achieve this higher rate of accumulation by higher collective saving resulting from the elimination of consumption by the capitalists, and to improve distribution by saving and investing collectively. (Robinson, 1955b, 17–18, 27).

However, the experience of a demographically fortunate Soviet Union could not be the relevant guide for overpopulated economies like China. Her own philosophy had evolved towards the position that a balance was necessary between population growth and the rate of capital accumulation merely to maintain the existing per capita income. The underdeveloped economies failed to do that; they were already in arrears:

> The level of real wages corresponding to the required rate of accumulation may be lower than the tolerable minimum. In such a case it is impossible for accumulation to keep up with population growth and a surplus of labour develops, in the sense that there is not enough capital to employ all available labour. The surplus grows until Malthusian misery checks the growth of population. "Underdeveloped economies" are those which have already got into arrears and have a surplus of labour relatively to the stock of capital goods. (Robinson, 1955a, 383)[3]

In the Malthusian situations like China, therefore, the problem of development required policy focus on accelerating capital accumulation as well on restraining population growth?[4] This had important implications for the choice of techniques. Before her second visit to China, Joan Robinson had been working on her *magnum opus* on capital accumulation (Robinson, 1956a). An important fallout of the preparatory work for it was her participation in an intense debate on the choice of techniques in the context of development or, to be more specific, Indian development. Mainly, she rejected what is known as the Dobb-Sen technique to maximise surplus per unit of investment and argued for a technique that would give maximum output per unit of investment. Its novelty lay in the implication that it would absorb relatively more labour also (Robinson, 1956b, c, d, e, 1957f). The significance of these discussions in the context of the Chinese development is not merely that they took place just before her visit to China in the autumn of 1957.

The year 1956 has a special significance in the history of socialist development. The workers of Poznan in Poland revolted against high-speed capital accumulation—the hallmark of Stalinism. What was later described anti-Stalin-Dobb-Sen technique (Hansen, 1975) was, according to Joan Robinson, "sometimes justified by appeal to the extreme hard- headedness of socialist policy, which enforces abstinence for the sake of accumulation. This argument has been weakened by the workers of Poznan, who demonstrated how hard-headedness may over-reach itself" (Robinson, 1956b, 9). She noted that some socialist countries "have been overdoing it", recognised "the excesses of Stalinism", but would not deny "its practical achievements" (Robinson, 1957c, 97, d, 159).[5] She was confident, like Baran (1957), that

> so far as the underdeveloped economies are concerned, it seems that socialism is going to beat capitalism at its own game, and the reason that it will do so is that it is a far more powerful instrument than capitalism for extracting the investible surplus from an economy. (Robinson, 1957c, 98).

In the month before her second visit to China, she declared:

> We know now that the problem of development can be solved by crowding the sweat and tears of two hundred years into a generation. We know that the communists do not suffer from legalistic inhibitions in dealing with landlords. We know that the incidentals of development—mass literacy, the freeing of women, the smashing of archaic customs—go fast enough with them. (Robinson, 1957e, 845).

The upshot thus far is that Joan Robinson had arrived at a set of conclusions about the Chinese development. Capital accumulation was the key to development. With a view to overcoming backwardness, China would need a high rate of capital accumulation. In As the conditions of backwardness and overpopulation, the relevant variable was the growth of capital per head. While capital accumulation had to accelerate, population growth was required to decelerate at the same time. As Lord Kahn recalled in his interview with the author (1 December 1986), basic reason for Joan Robinson's early interest in socialism was the possibility of accumulation at a desired level than under capitalism. Similarly, Adler confirmed Joan Robinson's confidence in the socialist state's "ability to foresee the future *en gros*" (1957, 63), which provided the basis for launching heavy industrialisation. However, in the process of pushing up its capital per head, Joan Robinson expected China to learn from the Soviet mistakes so as to minimise human costs. This was to be ensured by putting in place a system of planning and management—what she called a different set of the rules of the game—which would allow a smooth transition from private property in agriculture and industry, without being heedless of consumer demand.

State Accumulation, Technology and the Price System

These conclusions were reflected in the lectures given in China during her second visit in 1957 (JVR Collection, iii/5.1–5.3, King's College). As noted earlier, these lectures have not been published.

1. The Relations Between the Rate of Accumulation and the Price Level: In the first lecture on 4 September 1957 (JVR Collection), she argued for the superiority of the socialist rules over the capitalist rules in ensuring rapid capital accumulation. The "limits to pace of development" were set by (i) the digestive capacity of the economy and (ii) the amount of surplus in agriculture and manufacturing sectors. If capital goods were required to be imported, then the availability of exportable funds would limit the ability of the economy to digest investment. Given the digestive capacity, the limit to the pace of investment was set by the surplus realised from agriculture and manufacturing. Under capitalism, the limit implied that prices should move up and real wages should fall, with a reactive rise in money wages. There was also the problem of consumption out of profits in the manufacturing sector. The situation under socialism was stated to be different:

> In a planned economy you haven't got the problem of inflation because money wages are controlled. But you have got the problem of squeezing the people to a certain point without giving way. Therefore, this question of the pace of development involves a question of political judgement.
>
> Assume that the digestive capacity can be stretched. If it is larger than the surplus you can produce, then it is a question of how much surplus you can squeeze out and this is a question of political fact, therefore I doubt whether pure economic theory is useful in a planned economy. (JVR Collection, iii/5.1. King's College).

Joan Robinson set up the following simple numerical model to show the limits on the pace of development (Table 3.1).

The model assumes that the raw materials and consumer goods produced in agriculture are purchased by the official agencies at price 45 reckoned in some unit. It constitutes income accruing to (a). The output

Table 3.1 Limits on the rate of accumulation

	Agriculture (a)	Manufacture for Sale (b)	Social Outlay (c)	Investment (d)	
Income	45	25	10	20	= 100
Tax and profit	5	25	–	P*i*	–
Value of output	50	100	–	20 + P*i*	= 170 + P*i*

of (a) is the input for (b), while it is processed and sold to the public for 100. The income of this sector is 25. There is a gap of 30 between the total income (a) and (b) and the sales value of the output of (b), on which the whole of national income is assumed to be spent in the absence of personal saving. The gap is realised as taxes and profits which are spent on social outlay, yielding no profit, and investment. Profits and taxes ensure that the national product of 100 is not consumed entirely by (a) and (b). Joan Robinson treats profits that might be generated in the investment sector as mere book-keeping, so that P*i* does not enter the discussion. Similarly, the gross value of output, 170 + P*i*, has no bearing on her analysis.

Related to the political determination of the pace of development was the issue of allocating the burden between tax and profit from agriculture and income in the manufacturing sector—the terms of trade. Under capitalism, income in agriculture depends on prices while in manufacturing, prices depend on money income. A socialist economy had to exercise political judgement in this case as well. The criteria suggested included fairness and the provision of the right incentive. Robinson stated the riddle as follows:

> Sometimes we can provide more incentive, but it is not fair, such as squeezing the workers. These two purposes are of course not separated because feelings of fair dealing also provide incentive. You must find a solution which is fair and also gives incentive. (JVR Collection, iii/5.1. King's College).

Within agriculture, the quality of soil would cause unfair income differentials. With income depending on prices, equal amounts of work yield different incomes on different soil. Her solution was to introduce money rent and to "so arrange it that those working on better land will get the same income for an equal amount of work as those working on poorer land". What in time would have become a major source of inter-collective inequality was thus identified at the very beginning.

2. The Problem of the Choice of Technique for a Planned Economy with Limited Industrial Resources: In the second lecture delivered on 6 September 1957 (JVR Collection, iii/5.2. King's College), Robinson dealt with the question of the choice of techniques and how a Poznan-type situation may be avoided. She made the assumptions of surplus labour and scarce capital but rejected maximum employment as a criterion. Nor did she approve of the technique yielding greater output per head. However, the Dobb technique was considered most unsuitable for China:

> You want a large income for the next Five Year Plan, so you want to get an additional flow of output, that is, more surplus. If you use capital in a form which employs a lot of labour, you have got to allow those people to consume ... This is in a sense brutal theory. (JVR Collection, iii/5.2. King's College).

The image of China was being built up as a more humane economy. If it meant a shift from maximum surplus to no surplus, Joan Robinson was far from it. She was looking for an intermediate solution, already implicit in her idea of a superior technique. She repeated the distinctions between superior and inferior technique for the Chinese audience: "[T]he first distinction which has to be made is between those [techniques] which are superior and inferior and those which are less mechanized." It was during the visit to China that she made her position clear, suggesting that the choice of technique in China was consistent with her approach:

> The technique which will give the maximum profit is the same as that which makes the maximum contribution to your future surplus. Now some economists have argued for this maximum surplus as being the real object. I think they are overlooking the fact that additional wages are themselves a benefit. Potentially, a large output is that which leads to a large

surplus. The larger the total output the larger the potential surplus it contains. Therefore to look for a technique which will give the maximum profit is oversimplifying the question. On the other hand, to look for a technique which will give the maximum output is unrealistic. (JVR Collection, iii/5.2. King's College).

To illustrate the position, Fig. 3.1 was drawn. O/C indicates output per unit of investment and L/C is employment per unit of investment. The angle represents a constant wage rate and the curve indicates known technical possibilities. β technique is stated to be the Chinese choice because there is a surplus[6] of fβ and at the same time employment is higher by ab than the "Dobb method". The latter method is represented by D, which gives the highest surplus eD and the least employment Oa. At the other extreme is the maximum-employment and zero surplus technique, E, a "humanitarian" breakeven point.

The co-existence of the old and new techniques, noticed during the first visit (Robinson, 1954a, 33), was now stated to be "perfectly rational", as it involved "using superior technique in some enterprises because

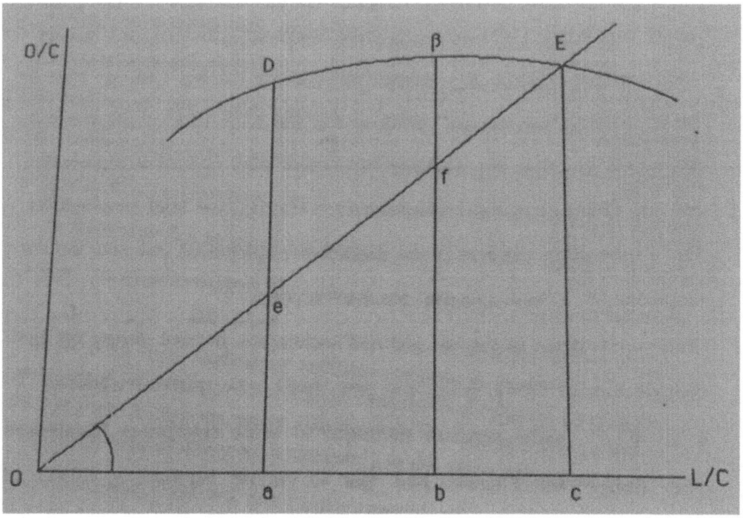

Fig. 3.1 The choice of technique in China. (Source: JVR Collection, iii/5.2, King's College, Cambridge)

in other things" the Chinese had "got to choose between a variety of techniques none of which are superior but some of which are more mechanised than others" (JVR Collection, iii/5.2). Later called "walking on both legs", Robinson believed the approach was consistent with rapid accumulation without imposing an intolerable sacrifice of consumption. In brief, the rate of accumulation and thus development would be higher under socialism than under capitalism due mainly to the advantage of political determination of surplus at the desired level. As noted above, she did not think that economic theory was of much use under socialism, insofar as the reinvestible surplus was concerned. This was not applicable to the population question:

> But at the same time I do think that economic theory is very useful in the socialist world. For instance, on the population question you have a very special question because there are very few places on the earth's surface which is [*sic.*] not over-populated. The Soviet Union is such a case and that gives a certain twist to their habits. (JVR Collection, King's College).

3. How Far and in What Way the Price System can be Useful in a Planned Economy: The third unpublished lecture delivered on 9 September 1957 addressed the all-important question of how to run the economy. Arrow has wondered why Joan Robinson had not been "sympathetic to" the school of socialist economists which "stressed the importance of the market".[7] He thinks she had "never shown any interest in how a socialist economy would operate, like Marx, but with less justification". The comment has not been made in all fairness. True, she did not construct a formal model of planning and management under socialism. Also, the unpublished lecture notes relevant to this topic end abruptly. But to say that she showed no interest in the way a socialist economy would work is not fully justified. She stated:

> It seems to me very strange that you find that you can use Marx's analytical apparatus in discussing problems of planned economy because Marx's analytical apparatus was built up in order to analyse capitalist economy in its early stage. It is appropriate to dealing with that particular kind of economy. It is very surprising if you can tailor-make that to fit to a totally different economic system. (JVR Collection, iii/5.3. King's College).

In considering the question of how any economy would operate, "what we have to look at is the means which has [*sic.*] to be used to make it run". Three types of mechanisms were available—legal, market and moral. The legal mechanism specified a set of administrative laws and procedures. Joan Robinson pointed out that it "has an advantage in that you can decide what is to be done and tell people to do it. But it has also very serious drawbacks, and when making complicated decisions it gets tied up in bureaucracy". This was the problem in Soviet Union. The market mechanism was based on self-interest, with agents "following the line which is going to give them a better return in money terms". She observed, profoundly:

> Now the market mechanism has very great merit in that it runs itself. Everybody is doing what he wants to do. This has really immense merits ... In the West the price system is always glorified as a means for maximum satisfaction, and it is criticised by many people that it does not give maximum satisfaction.
>
> This is really beside the point, its merit is not in maximizing anything, but in the fact that it will operate itself. It does not need any policing and does not need any bureaucrats, and that is enormous benefit. *This one comes to realise only by contrasting it with other systems* [Emphasis added]. (JVR Collection, iii/5.3).

Among the defects of the market mechanism were mentioned monopoly and a bad distribution of income. "So many of the evils of capitalist society are associated with the market system. The basic objection to capitalist society is its distribution of property. That is not necessarily the same thing, although it is historically connected with the market system."

As "perfectly egotistical behaviour is not possible, a moral code ... is an essential ingredient of any system". Mention was made here of loyalty to firm. The uniquely Chinese contribution consisted of a moral code—"a sort of proper behaviour is being developed in everybody and being formalized". Robinson considered it as "another way of running the economy". On a limited scale, its Western prototype was found in some professions, where a code of ethics was adopted for social rather than profit considerations. But the method had its problems. The difficulties of working out a moral code were one. More seriously, "people are not saints". Therefore, the "moral method can never operate alone, it has to be backed up by others", especially when the complexity of economic life increases. She put it to the Chinese:

> But as I see it, this development of the moral code I think is a unique contribution of China of another way of running the economy, and an extremely important contribution. What one would like to know is what will be the situation 20 or 30 years later when the main tasks are done and life is easier, then will be the difficult times. Your economy is still at an early stage, and the problem of administration gets more and more complicated as the level rises. When the question is to provide people with more food, more cotton, it is rather simple, and you know you need more steel, so providing a little more or a little less is not very important. (JVR Collection, iii/5.3. King's College)[8]

The question of prices under socialism was discussed more formally in Robinson (1958b) and its re-write, Robinson (1960e). *En route* to China in 1957, Joan Robinson had also gone to the Soviet Union, where the Khrushchev reform was being debated. She had the chance to discuss the questions involved with Soviet economists, who invited her to write a paper for the Soviet journal *Voprosi Ekonomiki*. As it appears, she had been reflecting on some of the issues raised in the lectures given in China for some time. Robinson (1958b) is the paper she wrote on the philosophy of prices, but the Soviet journal in question did not publish it (Robinson, 1975a, v). It contains all the important insights of her third lecture in China.

In a socialist system, she wrote, the objective was not "maximum satisfaction" but "a system of prices which will operate itself, without any need for rationing or any temptation to black marketeering". "The purpose was to lessen the resort to a bureaucratic system. Further, as workers were paid according to work done, it was analytically convenient to call the earnings of workers *wages*, and the excess of the receipts over costs in the operation of socialist enterprises *profits*." The requirements of the government to finance social outlays on non-saleable output determined overall profits and thus the relationship between prices and wages. In other words, it followed the sectoral distribution of burdens decided in the overall plan. Broadly, the pattern of final prices of commodities should follow the rule of balancing demand with available supplies. There was no unique pattern of prices, however. "A range of patterns of prices can all give an equally good fit with a given pattern of supplies. The pattern which happens to be ruling in any given situation must be largely a matter of historical accident." Like the pattern of final prices, the ex-factory prices must also be established by the planners. Leaving their prices to the enterprises would require additional administrative measures "to prevent them from behaving like capitalist monopolists". Joan Robinson did not approve of the general practice of fixing the final prices on a cost-plus basis, as it would act as a disincentive to cost minimisation, apart from the need to tell them "in great detail as to what to produce instead of having a simple motive to select the assortment of commodities within their range that yields the highest selling value per unit of costs". On the whole, "any scheme which makes a rational use of prices takes the weight off direct administration" (Robinson, 1958b, 130–2, 135).

Joan Robinson regarded "a fair distribution of income between agricultural and industrial workers" as the "major problem of price policy in a planned economy". To arrive at some desired distribution, she stressed the need to fix the farm prices below their demand prices so long as supply lagged behind demand. Its problems were recognised frankly.[9] A black market emerges if private sales are disallowed. If private sales are allowed, the "work-time and the use of land" shy away from selling to government. Even in the case of crops with no permissible private use and therefore running no risk of a black market, labour and land may be deflected to alternatives more lucrative than black or free market prices.

As in the lectures discussed above, Robinson favoured the principle of money rent, operating "like Ricardian rent" and mopped up as "land tax, assessed in terms of money instead of in terms of crops". To the extent that the land tax yield covers government expenditure, the need to mop up a surplus in the industrial sector would be reduced. It would thus be possible to ensure a desired inter-sectoral distribution of income. As the land tax was proposed to be levied according to the differential qualities of land, it would contribute to intra-sectoral equity in agriculture. According to her, these quality differentials were in the nature of property differentials; there was no justification for permitting the resulting income differentials (Robinson, 1960c, 33–6).

What emerges as the main point is that Joan Robinson considered China as a socialist economy, which would avoid the setting of detailed bureaucratic rules, use prices to take as much load off direct administration as possible and promote moral incentives in conjunction with other incentives. One has Samuelson's testimony on Joan Robinson's thinking on the necessity of market in the socialist economy of China[10] (their differences related to the market under capitalism).

Performance and Prospects at the End of the First Five-Year Plan

In *Economic Perspective* (Robinson and Adler, 1958), Robinson had the opportunity to judge the extent to which the economic development of China until the mid-fifties bore out her views. The visit by Joan Robinson took place at a time when the first five-year plan (1953–57) had been completed and discussions were afoot on the growth strategy of the second five-year plan.

First, the questions of rapid capital accumulation, the necessity of a socialist framework to achieve this rapidity and in a post-Poznan revision, the need to avoid overreaching the limits to accumulation and to respect consumer's sovereignty. In the first plan, the yearly accumulation/national income ratio was planned to be 21.6 per cent.[11] "Roughly 69 per cent of accumulation went into net investment in fixed assets—China doubled her stock of fixed capital in the four years 1953–56—and the remainder into building up working capital" (Robinson and Adler, 1958, 6). The sources of information were frankly admitted to be official, but the published statistics were found to be "reasonably consistent internally" and generally "conservative rather than otherwise" (*ibid.*, 3–4). By all accounts, China did achieve a very high rate of capital accumulation during its first plan. For the entire period of the first plan, Dong Fureng (1982) placed the ratio of accumulation to national income at 24.2 per cent. Not only was the rate of accumulation high, it was far above the average investment rate of 15–17 per cent estimated for the low-income countries in 1958 (Kuznets, 1966, 406). The average gross investment of over 21 per cent during the first five-year plan bore testimony to Joan Robinson's conclusion that the socialist rules of the game were more conducive to speeding up capital accumulation in backward countries than the capitalist rules. Despite being high, as well as higher than the economies following the capitalist path to development, the rate of accumulation in China was not considered excessive. The reason was

> the strong empirical bent of Chinese planners, who have so far, at any rate, successfully steered between the Scylla of too much accumulation with too slow an immediate improvement in living standards and the Charybdis of too little accumulation with too fast an immediate improvement in living standards. (Robinson and Adler, 1958, 6)

Having said that, the Chinese thinking was assessed to be inclined towards an accumulation rate "nearer 25 than 20 per cent" for the second five-year plan. It was stated in no uncertain terms:

> In any case, the projected rate of accumulation is hardly likely to fall below one-fifth of the national income, which is a very high rate by any objective standards. Industrialization and economic progress in agriculture on a scale and at a speed such as are being maintained in China are impossible without a high rate of accumulation. It is absolutely indispensable if the steep ascent from backwardness is ever to be completed, let alone accomplished in a reasonable span of time. (*Ibid.*, 7)

Thus if the peasants were not squeezed to the limit of impoverishment, urban workers enjoying a wage increase faster than the peasants during the first five-year plan were squeezed even less. The evidence in support is provided by many studies (Roll, 1974; Riskin, 1975). On the whole, "the increase in investment in the early to mid 1950s clearly did *not* result in *decline* in mass living standards" (Riskin, 1987, 77). The high rate of capital accumulation was financed through incremental growth in output, redistributive measures in industrial and commercial sectors, land reform and, not the least, by running a current account deficit with the

Soviet Union (Perkins, 1975, 176; Lippit, 1974; Eckstein, 1966, 126; Gurley, 1976, 163–4).

Apart from *Economic Perspective*, the population question was discussed in a separate article (Robinson, 1958a). It was noted that in the early "years after liberation the Chinese leaders turned a blind eye to the population problem". In "the Chinese setting this was peculiarly inept and now commonsense has prevailed over dogma". The demographic and economic elements of this common sense were identified, but there was no knowing "[h]ow far the Chinese discussion which was opened in 1955 followed these lines". First, there was a bulge in the rates of marriages and births after the establishment of peace under the People's Republic. Second, the demographic transition had occurred and China was "experiencing the typical explosion of population which takes place when a community passes out of the cruel primitive equilibrium of a high birth rate and a high death rate into a phase when the death rate has fallen and the birth rate remains at the primitive level". Infant mortality had been brought down, mainly by health and hygienic improvements. Third, the growth of numbers reduced land per head in agriculture. "The cultivable area of land could be greatly increased, but this is a capital investment competing with other investment schemes. If it is considered to be rewarding on its own merits there is no need to wait for an increase of numbers to undertake it." On the other hand, "if an increase in numbers [raising the overall demand for food] makes it obligatory, so much the less investment can be undertaken in industry or in social amenities." Lastly, the move from low-productivity occupations to high-productivity ones is counteracted by population growth. It was stated:

> Taking the pace of industrial development as given, the more labour there is to absorb from a growth in overall numbers, the longer it will be before mechanization to release labour from low-productivity occupations becomes possible. But that is not all. The pace of industrial development itself could probably be more rapid if numbers were smaller, for the agricultural surplus available for supporting investments and for export to purchase capital equipment is likely to be less the greater the number of mouths that have to be fed in the countryside. (Robinson and Adler, 1958, 17–18)

As noted above, it was far from certain whether the discussion started in 1955 followed up in any way her set of views on population. All the same, it was claimed: "Having decided that, both from the point of view of the national economy and from the point of view of the needs of individuals, birth control was to be desired, a nation-wide campaign was launched to popularize it" (*ibid.*, 19). As evidence of debate on the population problem was quoted a statement by Chen Po-ta in the People's China (16 March, 1956) to the effect that there was no overpopulation in China.

The pro birth-control view was attributed to Chen Yi and lifted from Sauvy (1957) (Robinson and Adler, 1958, 17). No direct interviews seem to have been held with the important participants in the debate. Yet Robinson believed that the "conclusion of the debate was favourable to birth control". As "the arguments in favour of birth control were victorious in the debate", what followed was an elaborate campaign which has now been in full swing for some time. In the campaign, "hostility is outweighed by eager acceptance". She was quick to admit, though: "Most of this I learned from an interview at the Ministry of Health, together with what casual checking up I was able to do". The summing-up was enthusiastic: "It is too soon to see the effect upon the figures. The next Chinese census will be exciting" (Robinson, 1958a, 66–7).

The Chinese demographers now see the period 1953–57 as one of the two population booms occurring in China under Mao (Tian Xueyuan, 1981, 35). With the exception of famine years, mortality fell and fertility rose throughout the fifties as well as the sixties (Banister, 1984, 718). While the 1953 census touched the 600-million mark, the 1964 census showed an addition of 100 million. Indeed, the official family planning programme did not start before 1962. The programme did not entail a clear-cut birth control policy. For political reasons, it was billed as a programme focusing on mother care. The Chinese demographers now confirm that this policy was "never really put into action" (Tian Xueyuan, 1981, 52). Robinson was correct in pointing out that the discussion on population was opened in 1955. In December 1954, Liu Shao-chi declared support of the party for birth control (Hou Wenruo, 1981, 60). The occasion was the 7th National

Congress of the Communist Party. It was, however, only in the following year at the 8th congress that the decision was made public.

Actually, the debate was a part of the "hundred flowers" policy. Among the opponents, Joan Robinson mentioned Chen Po-ta. What she failed to mention was that this person held the influential office of Mao's personal secretary. The supporters boasted the concurrence of Chou-En-lai, which is evident from his remarks made to the delegation of Indian agricultural planners in 1956. Neither the debate nor the campaign had any significant impact on the population growth (Perkins and Yusuf, 1984, 155–6; Government of India, 1956, 22–3; Aird, 1972, 227–75). By the time Joan Robinson arrived in China in the autumn of 1957, the "hundred flowers" policy had been halted, with which came to an end the resurgence of demographic research.

In terms of her lectures in China, the politically settled rate of accumulation would imply a desired apportionment of burdens between as well as within agricultural and industrial sectors. Robinson and Adler (1958) deals with these aspects inadequately and that too in an indirect way.

Joan Robinson had emphasised the crucial need for mobilising agricultural surplus for industrial development. According to other sources, the leadership in China was fully conscious of it (Walker, 1966, 3–4). Among the sources of finance for the high rate of accumulation, agricultural cooperatives were said to have contributed 10 per cent (Robinson and Adler, 1958, 6). Broadly, this corresponds to the contribution of agricultural taxes to the government revenue during the first plan period (Eclund, 1966, 20). However, she provided no clear clues to the more important transfer mechanism—the inter-sectoral terms of trade. The official index indicates consistent improvement in agriculture's terms of trade during the first plan period. This index has been criticised for its outdated coverage of the industrial items purchased by the agriculture sector (Riskin, 1987, 243–4). The criticism cannot apply to the early phase of the Chinese development, when the traditional industrial items included in the index could legitimately be believed to have formed the large bulk of industrial output sold to agriculture. A World Bank study also talks of net inflow of budgetary resources into agriculture as well as its favourable terms of trade vis-à-vis industry (Perkins and Yusuf, 1984, 13–26). Hence the claim that though the "Chinese countryside is extremely poor [,] an outsider returning to China after a number of years cannot but be impressed by the perceptible improvements in living standards".

This is not to say that agriculture was not squeezed; only that the squeeze was somewhat judicious. Rationing was introduced "not to curtail consumption below existing levels but to prevent it from rising too rapidly, so that too many of the gains of increased production do not go into increased consumption and too few into accumulation" (Robinson and Adler, 1958, 10–11). Clearly, Joan Robinson did not share the view expressed, for example, by Eckstein (1966, 30) about the impoverishment of the peasants during the first five-year plan period.

Ashbrook's (1975, 22) description—"[s]tabilization of living standard at Spartan but improved levels"—comes closest to her story. A more recent study finds persistent improvement in agriculture's terms of trade even over the longer period of 1952–1983. Any squeeze through the underpricing of agricultural products was thus more than counterbalanced.[12]

Intra-sectoral inequalities in agriculture, which in China took the form of inter-collective inequalities, have been found to be serious.[13] This did not escape Joan Robinson's attention, as this candid statement shows:

> By reason of their proximity to the big cities, the agricultural producers' co-operatives we saw tended to concentrate on the cultivation of vegetables and to derive a substantial part of their total income from subsidiary occupations such as pig breeding and dairy farming. Their average annual family income was over 500 yuan, whereas the national average for all co-operatives is somewhat over 300 yuan per peasant household, the lowest being a little over 200 yuan. These figures do not include incomes from individual subsidiary occupations or from cultivation of the small individual plots owned by all member families. Family plots are larger than one had expected to find, indeed they are big enough to provide a family with all its vegetables and sometimes a part of its cereals too. (Robinson and Adler, 1958, 7)[14]

Her advice to the Chinese to introduce rent or land tax to even out the differences between cooperatives in regard to fertility, access to markets, nature of crops and the intensity of exploiting private plots had gone unheeded.

To Joan Robinson, a peasant squeeze of East European proportions was not in evidence. As noted above, this was confirmed by other observers, too. Nor did she think that the industrial sector was acting on the Dobb-Sen technique to push the workers to the limits of riots *a la* Poznan. It was admitted that "working-class living standards are still undoubtedly very low". Further, the gap between the highest and the lowest urban incomes is "not very wide", but it exists. Nevertheless, the overall situation was one of improvement:

> The increase of around two-fifths in per capita money wages during the First Five-Year Plan, the establishment of the principle of equal pay for equal work, the eight-hour day, the great improvements in factory working conditions and the provision of basic amenities in the way of housing, health and education, have all contributed to a striking advance in working-class living standards. (*Ibid.*, 13)

It should be clear by now that Joan Robinson (a) considered collectivisation of agriculture as necessary, but expected it to be gradual, voluntary and smooth; (b) envisaged private capitalism in some industries to continue to play a useful role and (c) found moral incentives to be desirable but not sufficient; the market mechanism had a role to play. Some important events in the process of Chinese development in the fifties are discussed next to ascertain their impact on Joan Robinson's views on socialist development.

Some Important Events and Joan Robinson's Point of View

Before Joan Robinson's second visit in 1957, the most important event in China was "the high tide of socialism" unleashed during 1955–56. *Economic Perspective* does not reflect the dramatic pace of the changes involved. Within a matter of a year, peasant farming was eliminated and the process of forming cooperatives completed.[15] True, Joan Robinson had visualised land reform as only a step towards collectivisation. But she had also hoped that it would not be so sudden and reminiscent of the coercion associated with the collectivisation experience elsewhere. Some problems were admitted, but by the time she arrived, "the co-operatives we saw seemed to have pretty well overcome their teething troubles", the small number of peasants who quit earlier were rejoining and the "one solitary exception" refusing to rejoin had no doubt that his children would. Thus "the agricultural producers' co-operatives have finally put an end to the minute fragmentation of the land". The operational results were also found to be encouraging:

> Collectivisation in the co-operatives we visited had generally resulted in increases in the number of work-days per year, in land under irrigation and therefore also the index of double cropping, in land reclaimed, in productivity per *mou* (=0.1647 acre) and in incomes per family. While there were variations in all these increases as between the different co-operatives, the general upward movement was quite marked and in some cases striking. (*Ibid.*, 3, 8–9)

Whatever was left of private enterprise in industry, as well as the bulk of it in trade and commerce, drowned under "the high tide of socialism" in about a year. *Economic Perspective* notes in passing "an increasing tendency towards decentralization" in industrial planning and the "advantages possessed by a society in which capitalism had not taken deep root before its transition to a Communist way of life" (5, 14). Such a radical transformation had been accepted in sharp contrast to the earlier position, according to which the Chinese were not "root-and-branch" objectors to capitalism, nor were they inclined towards "an overhasty rush towards socialism".

It seems that in the quick elimination of peasant farming and private enterprise in industry, Robinson saw confirmation of her more general view that socialism as a development strategy was superior to the capitalist strategy. The pace of capital accumulation was higher under it: "Even upon cautious estimates, the rate of growth of industrial capacity is probably the most rapid the world has ever known" (Robinson, 1960d, 410). Such indeed it was, with the accumulation rate jumping to as high as 40 per cent during the Leap. It also meant that living standards stagnated after 1957 (Riskin, 1987, 109). The lessons of Poznan were forgotten. The excesses of capital accumulation were justified. From the advantages of not having a capitalist past the emphasis shifted to problems caused by it:

> Meanwhile socialism has come into being just in those countries that missed the capitalist bus. The tough, disagreeable aspects of socialism, which have so much weakened its idealistic appeal, are due precisely to this fact. Instead of expropriating the expropriators and settling down to civilized ease, the revolutionary governments had to lay upon their people hard tasks and curb their disillusion by bitter means. (Robinson, 1961b, 270)

Besides having "to carry out industrialisation for themselves', the socialist economies "have to contend with feudal property relations and ancient ideologies which capitalism failed to break down". Looking at "the relatively slow economic development of India … contrasted with that of China, Joan Robinson held that "Western liberalism has only warmed the surface of the deep waters of Indian tradition, while in China a violent reversal of ideas has opened the way for rapid changes in technology and in the social forms appropriate to exploiting them" (Robinson, 1962a, 106, 111). In regard to the socialisation of agriculture in China, she had now found an explanation for the "tremendous speed", which on her earlier view was fraught with the dangers of the Russian collectivisation experience. Now she thought that "there is a big difference between the agricultural problems in Europe and in China: the Chinese peasants seem really to have wanted co-operation."[16] Two reasons were advanced. For one thing, she repeated her earlier argument against land reform and for cooperatives; the high population density implied very small holdings as a result of land reform. For another, cooperation had been learned during the joint efforts for irrigation.[17] So conceived, it was more or less smooth sailing from land reform to mutual aid teams, lower forms of cooperatives based on the principle of "to each according to his land and work", then higher forms run on the principle of "to each according to his work" and, finally, to the communes organised as multi-dimensional self-reliant communities. But Robinson found the large size of the cooperatives to be problematic (Robinson and Berger, 1961, 220–2).

The "primary interest" of *Economic Perspective* was "in China as a functioning economy and in China's response to the long-term problems of industrialisation and the growth of population". It was published after the Leap, yet no need was felt to revise it. Joan Robinson, who had absorbed the shock of "the high tide of socialism", first discounted the possibility that even more fundamental structural changes could be sweeping across China so soon. It was predicted, naively, of the "events of 1958":

> The basic pattern of the Chinese economy had already been set in the period of "the high tide of socialism" in the winter of 1955–56 when the majority of Chinese peasants entered agricultural producers' co-operatives and when the private industrial sector was transformed into "joint State and private enterprises". This pattern, it is safe to predict, will persist during the Second and Third Five-Year Plans with, of course, a continued trend towards fuller socialisation of the joint sector. (Robinson and Adler, 1958, 20)

The Leap was an attempt to achieve the results of two five-year plans within a few years. At a time of planning chaos, Robinson wanted to know from Berger whether the Chinese were "running now, as they are in Russia, on a long-range plan, or is it going from five years to five years?" (Robinson and Berger, 1961, 222). At that point at least, the Leap did not seem to her important enough to influence China's course as a functioning economy. The Great Leap in industrial output was seen merely as further evidence of the cobweb-type unevenness in the rate of industrial growth, with high annual growth rates followed by low growth rates and a tendency to overcorrect them. The Great Leap in agricultural output was judged at least "roughly" feasible, implying a wider margin between food supply and population growth and thus leading "greatly to simplify the problem of long-term planning". It was also stated:

> There was a certain retreat, wasn't there? First they exaggerated the figures of the crop yields and then one heard stories of the breakdown of transport, everybody madly producing steel and not sending food into the towns, and this kind of thing. (Robinson and Berger, 1961, 221)

Berger explained away the exaggerated claims as well as the retreat as "a certain disbalance in the economy". Joan Robinson, however, understood that shifting enormous quantities of labour to producing steel in the backyard was bad economics:

> It may have been psychologically right, even if from the immediate economic point of view it was wrong. Getting everybody worked up into a tremendous state of enthusiasm about producing steel, for instance—perhaps from an economic point of view they would have been better producing something else; but this getting everybody involved was really the secret of how they had succeeded. (Robinson and Berger, 1961, 221)

The Leap put a sudden end to even the mild propaganda campaign for the control of population. The reasoning given out by the Chinese was that China was facing a scarcity of labour not a surplus, and population growth would help relax this scarcity. Joan Robinson found the proposition to be flawed. Even if the scarcity of labour existed, a high birth rate could not help: "If the women are having babies they are not able to help production—the manpower will become available in sixteen or twenty years' time when the whole economic situation will be completely different and meanwhile it must set more strain on the economy". Given the tremendous pace of economic growth attributed to the Great Leap by the Chinese, Joan Robinson seemed willing to concede on population that "they may not regard it as a menace but I don't see why they should regard it as a gain" (Robinson and Berger, 1961, 222). It was not difficult to see—and in terms of Joan Robinson's own line of argument. As noted above, she was not convinced about the economic case for shifting massive amounts of labour to small-scale steel production. A one-shot transfer of agricultural surplus labour to nonagriculture activity had occurred, creating the illusion of labour scarcity.

When the Chinese were pushing self-sufficiency at all levels, Joan Robinson considered it "a fallacy to suppose that as countries industrialize they become self-sufficient and reduce trade". Small industries may be developed within the communes, but she continued to believe that "the big modern installations are the backbone". She seemed unconvinced that the scale of operations under the communes was more natural than under the cooperatives. Indeed she was interested in urban communes as much as she was in agricultural communes. Some activities like irrigation in agriculture and the care and education of children in towns required such a collective effort (Robinson and Berger, 1961, 220–2).

In terms of lectures in China, as in Robinson's writings in general, the distinction between capitalism and socialism rested essentially in the ownership of property[18]; it had nothing whatever to do with the price mechanism. But

> as far as agriculture is concerned, it is technically advantageous to have a system of self-employment in which the cultivator is working for his own profit, because it is very difficult to organise labour in agriculture. This is the reason why the agricultural record in socialist countries is very poor compared to their record in industry. *Socialism is very much better fitted to industry than to agriculture* [Emphasis added]. (Robinson, 1963a, 9)

Once prices are disentangled from individual ownership, Joan Robinson believed that the distributional ailments of price mechanism do not follow. Their role then is in organising production efficiently. In socialised industry, price covering cost would not serve the purpose of development, which requires profits to finance further investment. Nor would development be served by allowing enterprises to fix prices due to the dangers of monopoly and inefficient operations. "The ideal system would be one in which the prices are given to the enterprises and it is their business to lower the costs and to make as large profits as possible." But there would still be the problem of why enterprises should strive to make large profits only to turn them over to the state. This is where the concept of loyalty to the firm, mentioned in the third lecture in China, was re-asserted (Robinson, 1963a, 8–12). She talked of "a strong propensity in human nature … for the individual to cotton on to any kind of group of which he finds himself a member". Nation, class, firm "evoke loyalty". Its strength in the case of firms "has falsified Adam Smith's prediction that joint-stock enterprise would be impossible, and Marshall's dictum that limited liability companies stagnate" (Robinson, 1962a, 133–4).[19]

Joan Robinson's lectures fitted well in the framework of the debates during the "hundred flowers" movement that followed the "high tide of socialism". The period between early 1956 and mid-1957 has been described as the rightist interlude of leniency, flexibility and adjustment (Vogel, 1969, 181–2). The overcentralisation of economic management was keenly debated. The rightists held views on the market, agricultural collectivisation, socialisation of industry and population growth which were not very different from those expressed by Joan Robinson in her lectures in China. Mao's speech on Ten Great Relationships in April 1956 had hinted at enterprise autonomy, but its overriding message was decentralisation towards lower levels of the government and the party. In September 1956, commerce minister Chen Yun advocated a position whereby the production and distribution decisions and the enterprise incentives would be so organised as to reflect, to some extent, the market considerations. Much like Joan Robinson's emphasis on the market as supplementing other mechanisms, Chen Yun argued for "three mainstays and three supplements": individual enterprises supplementing state and collective ownership, free production supplementing planned production and limited free market supplementing the state market. Chen Yun also proposed a return to the 1953 distribution system, which had won the acclaim of Joan Robinson. Essentially the system gave priority to commercial departments' purchases, but left the balance of the commodities for the market. Liu Shao-chi proposed circulation of even some capital goods on the market. Deng Xiaoping was concerned to find ways of overcoming bureaucracy in industrial enterprises. In her lectures, Joan Robinson had described bureaucracy as the main problem of the legal method of running the economy. During these debates, Mao had been stressing the law of value, which Joan Robinson always criticised as a piece of dogmatic Marxism. Ma Yin-chu advocated a strong population programme, which was an abiding concern of Joan Robinson. A number of economists questioned the relevance of Marx's analytical apparatus to the planned economy of new China. Joan Robinson had taken a similar position in her lectures.[20]

The actual course of events indicated decentralisation towards regional and local levels. Joan Robinson took note of it without much discussion. More important, the role envisaged by her for prices and incentives in her lectures in China in 1957 was not as much in evidence as she would have thought. "On the whole, the Chinese seem to prefer not to rely on price incentives in the production of major crops and to confine them rather to side-occupations, such as pig- and chicken-breeding, animal husbandry and the like." She reported "a combination of ethical appeals and price incentives" and the fact that "in the first period of collectivization the co-operatives tended to concentrate exclusively on grain to the detriment of side-occupation products". However, she was satisfied that "there is no doctrinaire reluctance to use price incentives where necessary; soya beans and cotton are outstanding examples of major crops whose prices were raised in order to stimulate production". These observations pertained to agriculture and related commerce. There is no discussion of prices in the context of industrial enterprises, except the attention paid to the drawbacks of interest-free working capital (Robinson and Adler, 1958, 5, 10, 12).

Joan Robinson lectured in China when the "hundred flowers" had ended and the anti-right campaign was underway. At the time, however, neither in the text of *Economic Perspective* nor in its postscript, which took a cursory note of the Leap, did she make any mention of it. An extremely difficult period for intellectuals (Macfarquhar, 1974, 314–15), it would have been cruel to name any names.[21] She waited until the rightist comeback in the post-Leap recovery period to refer to the rectification campaign.[22] In a review of Bowie and Fairbank (1962), she noted the birth control campaign was discontinued in 1958 and that "a professor got into serious trouble for his 'Malthusian' view". It was also observed that 1957 was "the 'high tide' of education in birth control" and it was gaining strength again (JVR Collection, ii/45, King's College). The aforementioned professor was Ma Yin-chu, whose views were part of a rightist economic consensus on how to move forward from the first five-year plan. He was the lone crusader for birth control after the "hundred flowers" movement. His *New Theory of Population* had been published in July 1957; it dealt with adverse effects of population growth on capital accumulation, productivity and living standards in the absence of an active family planning programme (Liu Suinian and Wu Qungan, 1986, 227).[23] Joan Robinson, as was seen above, held similar views.

Thus, when she "shook hands with Chairman Mao on the balcony of Tien An Men" on 1 October 1957 (Robinson, 1977b, 39), she had not yet become a Maoist. China was an overpopulated economy and the principal contradiction at the end of the first five-year plan was between economic backwardness and economic potential. Clearly emphasising the development of productive forces, she believed that the economy of China was "well on the way to surmounting the hump of the first and the hardest stage of industrialization" (Robinson and Adler, 1958, 20). The broad parameters of economic development were laid out in the unpublished lectures on China—capital accumulation at a humanly possible rate, birth control, some concern for consumer's sovereignty, economic management avoiding the bureaucratic tendency, selective use of prices and some role for moral incentives. The writings of the first phase survived the self-critical mood of the third phase. These writings and the unpublished lectures place Joan Robinson on the side of the rightists. The next chapter deals with the phase when she wrote more romantically than would make sense to many.

Notes

1. Joan Robinson was a left Keynesian by self-declaration (Robinson, 1953a). She wrote three pamphlets on the need for planning under capitalism (Robinson, 1943b, c, d). However, as planning did not follow a revolution in this case, it could not be "fully rational" due to the continued existence of "innumerable private rights and privileges" (Robinson, 1943d, 20–1).
2. For her weariness of Hegel, see Robinson (1953a, 20–3).
3. Robinson (1955a) is the same paper that was circulated in mimeographed form at a workshop in Poona (India) in June 1955 under a different title—"Pure Theory of Development". I am grateful to K. N. Prasad, who participated in the workshop, for sending me a copy of the paper bearing that title. Letters from K. N. Prasad, 29 September 1986 and 4 February 1987.
4. She wrote her paper on population and development (Robinson, 1960b) for an economic seminar at Moscow University, held in the month before her second visit to China in 1957.

5. Dalton (1974, 114) quotes Stalin and Joan Robinson together to convey the similarity of the message regarding capital accumulation in a socialist society. However, she considered Dobb to be a lackey of Stalin. As for herself, she had demanded to know in Poland in the presence of the top brass: "why are we wasting our time on [toasts and speeches] when the workers in Posen [*sic.*] are rebelling? What is the reason for that?" See Samuelson in Feiwel (1989, 135).
6. Joan Robinson's approach on surplus mobilisation and the choice of techniques in developing economies is similar to that of Kalecki. See Kalecki (1955, 1976, 55).
7. In Feiwel (1989, 178–9). See also Arrow (1953) for an earlier critique. Robinson (1960c) reflects her lectures in China.
8. Ten years on during the cultural revolution, she was made to believe that people could be saints and serve each other selflessly. In another ten years, she reverted to her original position that the moral method cannot run a complex economy. See Chap. 4.
9. She tended to minimise the significance of these problems when they actually arose during the rush towards collectivisation. See Chap. 4.
10. Feiwel (1989, 123) and Turner (1989, 131). See Robinson (1965a, 10) for her agreement with Solow on the relevance of some aspects of perfect competition theory and the concept of marginal productivity in planned economies.
11. National income here is the socialist concept, roughly the equivalent of the Western concept of net domestic material product.
12. See Yuming Sheng's doctoral dissertation, University of Cambridge (1989).
13. See Nolan (1983c) for an in-depth study of the problem. See also Nolan and White (1979).
14. Later she would deny the significance of private plots. See Chap. 4.
15. Those counselling caution were criticised by Mao as behaving like "a woman with bound feet". See Mao Tse-tung (1955).
16. The point was made about Cuba also in the same year: "Fidel insists that no request to set up a smallholder's cooperative should be met at the first asking. They must show that they really want it. No one is to be given an excuse to start talking about compulsory collectivization" (Robinson, 1961a, 266).
17. A third reason, given earlier, was the experience of some peasants who first quit and then rejoined the cooperatives when they found their

earnings to have fallen as individual cultivators (Robinson and Adler, 1958, 9).

18. Under capitalism there is "a continuous conflict over the question of who has a right to the surplus. The conflict does not arise in a socialist system" (Robinson, 1963a, 7). See also McFarlane (1982, 143).
19. See JVR Collection, iii/5.3. King's College. In this respect, Joan Robinson's thinking also influenced the theories of managerial capitalism and the corporate state. See Marcus (1967, 2, 1972, 113).
20. See Liu Suinian and Wu Qungan (1986, 183–5, 220–1, 227), Schumpeter (1968, 197–8), Riskin (1987, 100–8) and Goldman (1987, 244). See also Dong Fureng (1988, 242) and Lardy (1988, 254) on the strategy prescribed by the rightists to move forward from the first five-year plan.
21. She observed that Terrill's (1972) "habit of quoting conversations will mean that some people will be shy when he meets them again" (Robinson, 1972b, 321).
22. She recalled it much later as "the period of a campaign against rightists, which succeeded the 'hundred flowers'" (Robinson, 1977b, 38).
23. Later, Ma Yin-chu was dubbed a neo-Malthusian and a rightist and was sacked.

References

Unpublished Material

Interview with Lord Kahn, 1 December, 1986.

Yuming Sheng (1989) Intersectoral Resource Flows in Development Economics with Special Reference to China. Doctoral dissertation, University of Cambridge.

Published Works

Adler, S. (1957) *The Chinese Economy*. London: Routledge and Kegan Paul.

Aird, John S. (1972) 'Population Policy and Demographic Prospects in the People's Republic of China,' in *People's Republic of China: An Economic Assessment. Joint Economic Committee, Congress of the United States (1972)*, 220–331. Washington, DC: U.S. Government Printing Office.

Arrow, K.J. (1953) 'Review of Robinson (1951a),' *Econometrica*, 21, 621–3.

Ashbrook, Arthur G. Jr. (1975) 'China: Economic Overview,' in *China: A Reassessment of the Economy. Joint Economic Committee, Congress of the United States. China (1975)*, 20–51. Washington, DC: U.S. Government Printing Office.

Banister, J. (1984) 'Population Policy and Trends in China, 1978–83,' *China Quarterly*, 100, 717–41.

Baran, P. (1957) *The Political Economy of Growth*. New York: Monthly Review Press.

Bowie, R.R. and J.K. Fairbank. (eds.) (1962) *Communist China, 1955–1959: Policy Documents with Analysis*. Cambridge, MA: Harvard University Press.

Dalton, G. (1974) *Economic Systems and Society*. Harmondsworth: Penguin.

Dong, F. (1982) 'Relationship between Accumulation and Consumption,' in Xu Dixin, et al. (eds.), *China's Search for Economic Growth*. Beijing: New World Press.

———. (1988) 'Development Theory and Problems of Socialist Developing Economies,' in G. Ranis and T.P. Schultz (eds.), *The State of Development Economics*, 228–53. Oxford: Basil Blackwell.

EcKstein, A. (1966) *Communist China's Economic Growth and Foreign Trade*. New York: McGraw-Hill.

Eclund, G. (1966) *Financing the Chinese Government Budget: Mainland China, 1950–1959*. Chicago: Aldine.

Feiwel, G.R. (ed.). (1989) *Joan Robinson and Modern Economic Theory*. London: Macmillan.

Goldman, M. (1987) 'The Party and the Intellectuals,' in R. Macfarquhar and J.K. Fairbank (eds.), *The Cambridge History of China*, Vol. 14, 218–58. Cambridge: Cambridge University Press.

Government of India. (1956) *Report of the Indian Delegation to China on Agricultural Planning and Techniques*. New Delhi: Government of India Press.

Gurley, J.G. (1976) *China's Economy and the Maoist Strategy*. New York: Monthly Review Press.

Hansen, B. (1975) 'Review of R. Findlay, International Trade and Development Theory in,' *Journal of Development Economics*, 1, 403–4.

Hou Wenruo. (1981) 'Population Policy,' in Liu Zheng, et al. (eds.), Liu Zheng, et. al. (1981) *China's Population: Problems and Prospects*. Beijing: New World Press, 55–76.

Kalecki, M. (1955) 'The Problem of Financing Economic Development,' *Indian Economic Review*, 2(3), 1–22.

———. (1976) *Essays on Developing Economies*. Hassocks, Sussex: Harvester Press.

Kuznets, S. (1966) *Modern Economic Growth: Rate, Structure and Spread*. New Haven: Yale University Press.
Lardy, N.R. (1988) 'Comments on Deng Fureng,' in G. Ranis and T.P. Schultz (eds.), *The State of Development Economics*, 254–9. Oxford: Basil Blackwell.
Lippit, V. (1974) *Land Reform and Economic Development in China*. White Plains, NY: International Arts and Science Press.
Liu Suinian and Wu Qungan. (eds.) (1986) *China's Socialist Economy: An Outline History*. Beijing: Beijing Review Press.
Macfarquhar, R. (1974) *The Origins of The Cultural Revolution. 1: Contradictions among the People 1956–1957*. London: Oxford University Press.
Mao Tse-tung. (1955) 'On the Cooperative Transformation of Agriculture,' in *Selected Works*, Vol. 5, 184–207, 1977. Peking: Foreign Languages Press.
Marcus, R. (1967) *The Economic Theory of 'Managerial' Capitalism*. London: Macmillan.
———. (1972) 'Is the Corporate Economy a Corporate State?,' *American Economic Review, Papers and Proceedings*, 62, 103–15.
McFarlane, B. (1982) *Radical Economics*. New York: St. Martin's Press.
Nolan, P. (1983c) *Growth Processes and Distributional Change in a South Chinese Province: The Case of Guangdong*. London: Contemporary China Institute.
Nolan, P. and G. White. (1979) 'Socialist Development and Rural Inequality: The Chinese Countryside in the Seventies,' *Journal of Peasant Studies*, 7, 3–48.
Perkins, D.H. (1975) *China's Modern Economy in Historical Perspective*. Stanford University Press.
Perkins, D.H. and S. Yusuf. (1984) *Rural Development in China*. Baltimore: The Johns Hopkins University Press for World Bank.
Riskin, C. (1975) '"Workers" Incentives in Chinese Industry,' in *China: A Reassessment of the Economy*, 199–224. Congress of the United States, Joint Economic Committee. Washington, DC: U.S. Government Printing Office.
———. (1987) *China's Political Economy: The Quest for Development Since 1949*. New York: Oxford University Press.
Robinson, Joan. (1943a) 'Review of Schumpeter (1943),' *Economic Journal*, 53, 381–3.
———. (1943b) *The Future of Industry*. London: Fredrick Muller.
———. (1943c) *Private Enterprise or Public Control*. London: The English Universities Press.
———. (1943d) *The Problem of Full Employment*. London: The Workers' Educational Association and Workers' Educational Trade Union Committee.
———. (1949) 'Theory of Planning,' Review of M. Dobb. *Soviet Economic Development Since 1917, Soviet Studies*, 1, 60–4.

———. (1951a) *Collected Economic Papers*, Vol. 1. Oxford: Basil Blackwell.
———. (1951b) 'Preparation for War,' Reprinted from *Cambridge Today* in *Monthly Review*, 3, 194–5.
———. (1952a) 'Theory and Practice of Planning,' Review of C. Bettelheim, *Problemes Theoriques et Pratiques de La Planification, Soviet Studies*, 4, 53–8.
———. (1953a) *On Re-reading Marx*. Cambridge: Students' Bookshops.
———. (1954a) *Letters from a Visitor to China*. Cambridge: Students' Bookshops.
———. (1954b) 'Britain and China,' *Nation*, 179, 125–8.
———. (1955a) 'A Theory of Long-run Development,' *Economic Review*, October 1955a, 6, 382–5.
———. (1955b) *Marx, Marshall and Keynes*. Delhi: Delhi School of Economics, Occasional Paper No. 9.
———. (1956a) *The Accumulation of Capital* 1st ed. London: Macmillan.
———. (1956b) 'Unemployment and the Second Plan,' *Capital*, Annual Supplement, 7–9. Reprinted in Robinson (1965a), 182–91.
———. (1956c) 'Employment and the Plan,' *Economic Weekly*, 8, 355–6.
———. (1956d) 'The Choice of Techniques,' *Economic Weekly*, 8, 715–18.
———. (1956e) 'Time and the Choice of Technique,' Comment on Chakravarty (1956), *Economic Weekly*, 8, 1333.
———. (1957c) 'Notes on the Theory of Economic Development,' in Robinson (1960a), *Collected Economic Papers*, Vol. 2. Oxford: Basil Blackwell. 88–113.
———. (1957d) 'What Remains of Marxism,' in Robinson (1965a), *Collected Economic Papers*, Vol. 3. Oxford: Basil Blackwell. 158–66.
———. (1957e) 'The Indian Mixture,' Review of M. Zinkin. *Development for free Asia, New Statesman and Nation*, 54, 844–5.
———. (1957f) 'Choice of Technique,' Letter to *Economic Weekly*, 9, 537.
———. (1958a) 'Birth Control in China,' *New Statesman and Nation*, 55, 66–7.
———. (1958b) 'Some Reflections on the Philosophy of Prices,' *Manchester School of Economics and Social Studies*, 26, 116–35.
———. (1960b) 'Population and Development,' *Pakistan Economic Journal*, 10, 1–7.
———. (1960c) *Exercises in Economic Analysis*. London: Macmillan.
———. (1960d) 'Review of T.T. Hughes and D.E.T. Luard,' *The Economic Development of Communist China, Economic Journal*, 70, 409–10.
———. (1960e) 'The Philosophy of Prices,' in Robinson, 1960a, 27–48.
———. (1961a) 'From the United States to Cuba,' *Listener*, 66, 265–7, 80.
———. (1961b) 'Review of S. Tsuru (ed.),' *Has Capitalism Changed? Monthly Review*, 13, 265–71.

———. (1962a) *Economic Philosophy*. London: C.A. Watts.
———. (1963a) 'Public and Private Enterprise,' *Applied Economic Papers*, 1–12.
———. (1965a) *Collected Economic Papers*, Vol. 3. Oxford: Basil Blackwell.
———. (1972b) 'Through Western Spectacles,' Reviews of K. Mehnert, *China Today*; Terrill (1972); and K. Ling, *Red Guard, Spectator*, 7522, 321.
———. (1975a) 'Introduction 1974: Reflections and Reminiscences,' in *Collected Economic Papers*, Vol. 2, 2nd ed. Oxford: Basil Blackwell, iii–xii.
———. (1977b) *Reports from China, 1953–76*. London: Anglo-Chinese Educational Institute.
Robinson, Joan and S. Adler. (1958) *China: An Economic Perspective*. London: Fabian International Bureau, Fabian Tract No. 314.
Robinson, Joan and R. Berger. (1961) 'Thinking about China: The Economic Impact of Communism,' *Listener*, 2 February 1961, 65, 220–2.
Roll, C.R. (1974) *The Distribution of Rural Income in China: A Comparison of the 1930s and the 1950s*. Doctoral dissertation, Harvard University, Cambridge, MA.
Sauvy, A. (1957), 'La Population de la Chine,' *Population*, 12, 695–706.
Schumpeter, J.A. (1943) *Capitalism, Socialism and Democracy*. London: Allen and Unwin.
———. (1968) *Ideology and Organisation in Communist China*. Berkeley: University of California Press.
Terrill, R. (1972) *800,000,000: The Real China*. London: Heinemann.
Tian Xueyuan. (1981) 'A Survey of Population Growth since 1949,' in Liu Zheng, et al., *China's Population: Problems and Prospects*. Beijing: New World Press. 32–54.
Turner, M.S. (1989) *Joan Robinson and the Americans*. Armonk, NY: M.E. Sharpe.
Vogel, E.F. (1969) *Canton under Communism: Programs and Politics in a Provincial Capital, 1949–1968*. Cambridge, MA: Harvard University Press.
Walker, K.R. (1966) 'Collectivisation in Retrospect: The "Socialist Hightide" of Autumn 1955–Spring 1956,' *China Quarterly*, 26, 1–43.

4

The Second Phase: A "Starry-eyed" Joan Robinson

"Starry-eyed" was the expression used by Joan Robinson herself in the context of her controversial contributions on China (Robinson, 1982, 3). The phase during which these contributions were made started after the summer of 1963, when she undertook the third visit to China, and lasted until 1975. During this phase, the Chinese imposed a strict informational moratorium. It was therefore left to those presumed to enjoy direct access to the Chinese sources to analyse for the outside world the developments taking place in China. This chapter shows that she failed to do precisely that in a number of important respects.

The Famine That Never Happened

The third visit was an opportunity for her to find out what actually happened during the Leap and to analyse its impact. By the time she arrived in China, the communes themselves had undergone a change as a consequence of the difficulties of the Leap. Yet the impression that communes made on her mind was so deep that it diverted her attention from the question of probing a bit more the state of food availability during "the

P. Tahir, *Making Sense of Joan Robinson on China*, Palgrave Studies in the History of Economic Thought, https://doi.org/10.1007/978-3-030-28825-9_4

three bitter years". Like most China observers, Joan Robinson failed to appreciate that beneath the Leap over-optimism was concealed a famine of major proportions, now known to have claimed millions of lives (Coale, 1984, 66–70; Aird, 1982; Ashton et al., 1984). Before the visit, she understandably doubted the famine stories (Robinson and Adler, 1958, 20; Robinson and Berger, 1961, 222; Robinson, 1962a, 121, b, 734). The doubt became a flat rejection after the visit. She continued to believe that all the talk about the deteriorating grain situation was mere propaganda. Joan Robinson went to the extent of making the specific claim: "No one starved. This was an experience much more completely unprecedented than the natural disasters" (Robinson, 1964e, 286). Describing the breakdown of the communes during the Great Leap as a misconception, she asserted:

> I think the reverse is the truth. It was the existence of communes which made it possible for the authorities to see the country through. In the old days it would have been quite normal for ten or twenty million people just to die from starvation and millions more to disperse about the country becoming beggars in towns or living on roots in the woods. This time the whole country was looked after, communities were kept together, the bad areas were supplied with grain, the rationing system looked after the cities. In coping with these huge problems the organisation of the communes played an indispensable part. (Robinson, 1964b, 199)

Interestingly, she admitted the existence of "a complete statistical blackout". She could

> only guess, from the behaviour of rations and prices, and from the impressionistic evidence of talks in communes, that the grain output is now well above the level of 1957 (the exaggerations of 1958 are tacitly passed over on both sides), that current consumption is adequate, but that stocks have to be built up. (Robinson, 1964e, 297)

As it turns out, the guess was nowhere near the fact of the matter. The grain output was 195 million metric tons in 1957. In the year of her visit, 1963, it was 170 million metric tons. As she visited in summer, the relevant figures would be that of 1962, which stood at 160 million metric tons. "The 1957 level was regained only by 1965" (Perkins and Yusuf, 1984, 34). Needless to say, the impressions about consumption and stocks also left much to be desired. Far from relieving misery and preventing starvation, the Leap measures—communes in their original form included—first caused it and then obstructed relief. Exaggerated output figures led to official over-procurement; the resulting shortages in rural areas were concealed by cadres to justify claims. In 1960, the year of the lowest grain output, as much as 35.6 per cent was procured by the state. This was also the year of the highest mortality, recording a negative natural rate of increase. The labour transfer to nonagricultural pursuits, together with the natural calamities and other policy errors, led to the famine (Riskin, 1987, 136–8).

Joan Robinson had argued earlier that collectivisation was necessary to increase agricultural productivity. It would speed up mechanisation and thus make possible the release of labour from low- to high-productivity occupations (Robinson, 1954a, 28–9; Robinson and Adler, 1958, 17–8). Actually, collectivisation took place without any significant mechanisation and the labour transfer took place to rural industrialisation of doubtful productivity. To make the impact of the famine worse, migration to urban areas was obstructed. The rural labour's marginal product was low and falling but not zero (Perkins and Yusuf, 1984, 57). Obviously, the shift was at the expense of the production and transport of agricultural output. The output of grains plummeted, with the transport system unable to carry even the vastly reduced supplies of food. But she remarked:

> It was the communes that made it possible for the authorities to see the country through without the famines and massive deaths from starvation that were commonplace in the old days, and to keep the price of foodstuffs steady. (By the way, I think it was a more remarkable achievement than any "great leap" to have come through this period of severe shortages without inflation). (Robinson, 1964a, 178)

Her tone was now becoming propagandist:

> The commune system was thoroughly well put through the wringer during the three 'bitter years' of flood and drought that followed 1958 (when the

critics were shedding crocodile tears over the 'famine') and has emerged in a sensible, flexible and realistic form. (Robinson, 1964c, 6)

In fact, Brammall's (1989) detailed comparison of the famines in the early thirties and the early sixties shows the truth to be the reverse of Joan Robinson's contention. His study of Sichuan, the most populous province of China, finds that the famine in Mao's China had no counterpart in the thirties.[1] Later, Joan Robinson compared the conditions in China of the Leap with the Russian famine: "The historical analogue of this is the Russian famine of 1921" (Robinson, 1969f). The analogue failed to alarm her to the fact that "the two worst famines of the twentieth century … occurred under collective farming" (Nolan, 1988, 6).

Birth Control: The Return of the Orthodoxy

Joan Robinson also wanted to find out during her visit in 1963 whether "the birth control movement, in full swing in 1957, had been called off in a return to Marxist orthodoxy" (Robinson, 1964b, 195). She reported that the "authorities recognise that numbers are growing much too fast". They "have dropped their Marxist orthodoxy and look at the problem in a common sense way". It was also admitted: "The statistical blackout covers demography, but we are allowed to know that the overall numbers have not yet touched 700 million but soon will" (Robinson, 1964a, 179, b, 203, e, 297). As measures of population control, the Chinese "advocate late marriage and family planning" (Robinson, 1964f, 756).

Joan Robinson is here referring to the post-Leap or, to be more correct, post-famine attitude towards the problem of population. There was a revival of the birth control campaign during this period (Aird, 1972, 297), but the argument is presented as if the reversal of the campaign during the Leap never took place. Nowhere was it mentioned that the revival of the birth control campaign was associated with the regaining of control by the rightists.

During her fourth visit in October 1964, Joan Robinson noted that a population census had been taken, which "seems to have shown a disturbingly high rate of growth of population". Yet there was reluctance to discuss the population problem in the context of development and the propaganda campaign was "not perfectly candid" (Robinson, 1965c, 11–2).[2] She failed to note here the beginning of the end of the control of the rightists over policy-making. Later it was also admitted that policy makers had retreated from the birth control campaign during the Leap but that "since 1963 it has been going great guns" (Robinson, 1966e, 548). Writing in the same year, her enthusiasm about the success of the campaign dampened. At a time when no statistics were being published, she noted the guess made by Dumonr (1966) that the grain output in 1964 had regained the level of 200 million tons achieved in 1958. The addition to the population during the interval was guessed as 80 million. She found somewhat mysterious the reports from the visitors that, "judging by the eye, the Chinese population have never been so well fed". Joan Robinson wondered: "Perhaps the growth of numbers (as Mao told Edgar Snow) has been over-reported. Or perhaps the commune authorities wink at under-planning by the teams. Or perhaps the foreign economists under-estimate production." But her own view of the problem remained set: "However that may be, any growth of numbers is a serious burden on the Chinese economy" (Robinson, 1966g, 72).

The Leap in the Communes

The major outcome of visiting China in 1963 was neither the state of food nor population but a spate of studies on the organisation of the communes. Organisationally, the communes went beyond the concept of collectivisation in Eastern Europe, as well as Joan Robinson's own initial views on the socialisation of agriculture. As is shown in the following paragraphs, she went along with the new Chinese concept, believing it to be a path-breaking innovation in the organisation of agriculture: "the most interesting question to take up" (Robinson, 1964a, 177). In all 12 communes were visited in 5 different provinces[3] and an attempt was made to somewhat randomise the sample:

> I chose to visit places of historical and artistic interest and then asked to be taken to nearby communes, which provided me with a fairly random

> selection. Officials in Peking told me that some of the communes have gone badly wrong. I did not see one of those. But in my casual sample there was a great variety of types and of levels of success. Naturally, making visits relying on an interpreter one can get only superficial impressions, but all the same I learned a great deal. (Robinson, 1964a, 177)

In studying the communes, as in analysing the cooperatives in her second visit, Joan Robinson was searching for an appropriate scale of organisation for agriculture under conditions of high labour/land ratio and low capital/labour ratio. During her 1957 visit, when higher-form cooperatives had become general, she "found that the lack of previous managerial experience imposed fairly definite limits on economies of scale in the earlier stages". Given the limited mechanisation, "larger cooperatives had few inherent advantages over the smaller". Indeed, the cooperativisation led to "the apparent paradox that Chinese farming has become more and not less labour-intensive with collectivisation". Labour abundance and capital scarcity forced the progress of mechanisation to be slow. However, in areas involving externalities, such as the use of power for pumping and irrigation, cooperatives demonstrated the benefits of mechanisation (Robinson and Adler, 1958, 7–8).

The argument that cooperativisation had been learned in works involving externalities was noted above. Now it was claimed that land-creating investments provided the "original nucleus of the commune system" and one which "evolved into an ingenious system of reconciling the requirements of large and small scale" (Robinson, 1964d, 2, 4). Cooperatives were too large for labour deployment:

> For the deployment of labour, a rather small scale is required. Workers are spread out over space so that discipline is hard to enforce; an incentive wage system is not easy to arrange or to administer; there has to be a great diffusion of managerial responsibility; every field is different, every day is different and quick decisions have to be taken. For getting work out of the workers a peasant family is hard to beat. Discipline and responsibility are imposed by the pressing incentive to secure the family livelihood. (Robinson, 1964d, 1)

But the cooperatives were too small for the deployment of land to its best use, and the peasant

> family unit is much too small. Transport and marketing are costly; specialised production is worthwhile only for valuable cash crops. The bulk of consumption is provided for on the spot. The various products required must be raised on whatever land the family happens to command. (Robinson, 1964d, 1)

Both the labour and the land available to the cooperatives were "too small to exploit the possibilities of improvements through irrigation, drainage, afforestation and so forth". Similarly, the situations of knowledge deployment required a scale of operation beyond the cooperatives and well beyond the peasant operator, who cannot afford to risk his daily bread in experiments (Robinson, 1964d, 1–2).

The communes were organised into "a three-decker system"—the team, the brigade and the commune, which put each resource to its best use. There were variations and the deckers performed many functions other than those mentioned here, but the concern here is with what Joan Robinson considered to be the most important functions. Appropriate labour allocation was achieved through the team, which was the basic unit of accounting and distribution.[4] It was small enough to manage labour on a given land. The scale maintained the diffusion of responsibility required in agricultural operations as well as satisfied the dictum that "the economic incentive tells better in small unit than in a large one". About 40 per cent of the income grossed by the team went into the agricultural income tax, production costs, accumulation fund, welfare fund and a management fee to the commune. The balance of 60 per cent was distributed according to workpoints. The brigade consisted of a certain number of teams to which it allocated land according to a crop programme. The land allocation was thus performed on a scale larger than was required for labour allocation, ensuring the efficient use of labour as well as land. At the commune level, the appropriate economies of scale were reaped for large investment projects as well as rural industries besides the activities entailing externalities for the team and the brigade and economies external to the commune.

On the whole, "the commune offers to its members the 'five guarantees' of food, clothing, shelter, medical care, and funeral expenses, something like a Beveridge plan". Joan Robinson did not believe that the communes broke down during the three bad years. Nor did she find any truth in what some observers believed to be an attack on the family life. Family continued to be an important economic unit, "which makes the young people keen to earn and therefore work". The only thing that broke down was the "Utopian … idea of giving people their ration of food irrespective of the labour-days that they worked". Instead of seeing a link between the resistance of the family institution when it came under radical attack and the restoration of work-related earnings, Joan Robinson put a gloss over it by describing the recanting "as a kind of qualitative 'operations research'—the nearest thing of an application of the scientific method to economic policy that exists anywhere". On another occasion, it was described as "a concession to realism". When "there is a dispersion in earnings", a small group such as the team is preferable to a large group in that it makes "more visible … the connection between one's own effort and one's income". Her objection is not to personal "ambition [which] has scope to express itself in more constructive ways" in the commune system, but to "the desperate acquisitiveness of the individual peasant". She also stated: "Economic incentives are not everything; the authorities are much concerned to keep morale high, but they are careful not to put any more weight on it than it can bear" (Robinson, 1964a, 177–9, b, 199, c, 11, d, 2–5, e, 289, 295).

In sum, communes were considered to be a brilliant blend of individual incentive and collective advantage: "The team is small enough to bring individualistic economic incentives into play. The commune is large enough to exhibit the visible benefits of collective organisation." At the collective level, the greatest achievement was stated to be the saving and creation of land through cooperative effort. At the individual level, the provision of food, shelter and incentive goods was the chief merit (Robinson, 1964e, 295–6). "Personal ability and ambition" was not decried; the communes allowed its expression more constructively than the peasant acquisitiveness (Robinson, 1964c, 11).

In practice, the blend of individual incentive and collective advantage did not turn out to be as brilliant as Joan Robinson imagined. This comes out clearly from the work being done by Liu Minquan.[5] According to him, while this blend operates to the point of enlisting members for collective work, there is no mechanism to ensure that each member will supply the effort required.

Like production, marketing was also organised in three tiers. At the lowest tier, fairs were held, where supply and demand reigned freely to determine prices. The output sold originated in households and an occasional cart-load from the team. Robinson mentioned the household production to be around 10 per cent of the aggregate supply. Contrary to what she stated to be propaganda, the family continued to be an important social as well as economic institution under the communes, together with a thriving private economy following the supply-and-demand rules of the game in production as well as marketing. But the family plots were small; a six-member family had one-fifth or one-tenth of an acre. In addition, there were small vegetable gardens in the courtyards, with some fruit trees. The peasants also kept chickens and a pig or a goat. She mentioned "a general rule that the area set aside for them must not exceed 5 or 7 per cent of the whole". As the context states the team or the brigade as the allocator of the private plots, the percentages mentioned should apply to them (Robinson, 1964c, 8, d, 6, e, 290–1).

Robinson did not clearly bring out the fact that family did come under the radical attack in the beginning. Again, nowhere does she take note of the equally important fact that the private plots were first swept away under the revolutionary fervour revived only after the setbacks of "the three bitter years". Other writers were aware of this retreat as well as the critical feature that the "private plots … represent a far larger part of agricultural production than the 5 per cent of land to which they are restricted" (Hayward, 1966).[6] Walker attributes the decline of animal and poultry population to the decline of private plots (1965, 54–63).

The middle tier of the marketing was the supply of meat, vegetables or wines or hog bristles by the team or the brigade to the supply and marketing cooperatives for retailing in the village or nearby towns. Prices were fixed, bearing some relationship to costs (Robinson, 1964c, 8). It was the third tier that was the main tier of marketing:

> The main outlet for agricultural produce is through the state procurement agency, which has the sole right to handle the main crops. Deliveries are agreed in advance in the annual plan and prices have been held substan-

> tially unchanged since the currency stabilisation of 1950. Retail prices are also fixed. In some cases the margin is not sufficient to cover transport and handling charges, so that the urban population is partly getting its food below cost. Where a team is allotted some specialised work and has to buy its grain, purchases must be made through the sate organisation, though the grain may come physically from next door. (Robinson, 1964d, 6)

Cash crops could be sold to government agents at fixed prices in whatever quantities the communes had to offer. In regard to grain, the communes entered into an agreement with government agents at the start of the year as to planned output, the proportion to be retained by the communes and the surplus to be turned over at fixed prices. For fruits and vegetables, the problems connected with excess supplies were sorted out by general agreements between the cities and the communes about the quantities to be supplied, while teams entered into firm supply contracts with the shops for actual deliveries. Price to the consumer was lowered to clear the big summer crops, while the farmer got a guaranteed price; it was pushed up for early spring crop.[7] The "system gets over the problem, which plagues a market economy, of the farmer who hanged himself in the expectation of plenty" (Robinson, 1964a, 179). She believed it to be "very simple and sensible compared to the frustration and paradoxes of a market economy" (Robinson, 1964b, 203).[8]

While the discussion of marketing together with production distinguishes her from analysts who focus principally on the internal functional re-organisation of the communes, Joan Robinson's view is that marketing was structured by the organisational tiers of the communes. Skinner (1965, 395–9), however, suggests that the natural marketing systems that the commune movement had sought to abolish but which reasserted themselves during the disastrous years of the Leap shaped the re-organisation of the communes. Paradoxically, Skinner quotes as evidence the information given to Joan Robinson that "the system of teams, brigades and communes has been grafted on to the ancient roots of rural life" (Robinson, 1964c, 7).

After the fourth visit, Joan Robinson spoke of "the all-round turn for the better in the economy that set in last year", notably in agriculture, without analysing the real causes of the turn for the worse that had preceded it (Robinson, 1965c, 11). The sudden abolition of private plots, the free supply of food to each according to need, the backyard steelmaking and the over-sized units of account as were the communes have all had their contributions to make to the difficulties of the three bad years. She had the occasion to review Walker's (1965) study of private plots. However, she believed that the abolition of private plots was not as general as Walker made it look. "Like the "free supply" of food grains, it was one of the rather dotty experiments, launched in some of the communes during the Great Leap, which were quickly abandoned." Similarly, the retreat from the commune as a unit of account to the lower form was "a concession from theory to reality which was not always necessary". A study like Walker's, based as it was on a study of documents, had "a tendency to generalise". It had to be "corrected" by on-the-spot studies of specific communes, such as the work of Jan Myrdal (Robinson, 1966a, 159–60, 1968a, 152).[9] The "most enlightening" of all such studies was carried out by Crook and Crook (1965). The village visited by the Crooks had witnessed all the stages of the unit of account descending from the commune to the brigade and finally to the team. Robinson drew the conclusion: "By a process of adapting to experience, rather than by a priori analysis, the communes have now arrived at a good fit between the functions of the various levels of management and the economies and diseconomies of scale in the various spheres of production" (Robinson, 1966g, 70).

What Joan Robinson considered to be a great advantage of the commune system—creating land through community effort—was described by Dumonr (1966), a sympathetic visitor, as an extravagant use of labour. She found the argument to be inconsistent with the high labour/land ratio in China. "More cogent is Professor Wertheim's thesis, that the Chinese have succeeded in creating a scarcity of labour by substituting manpower for capital." What had appeared to her as a strange argument—scarcity of labour—before visiting China after the Leap, was now accepted as an achievement. According to her, the work such as an irrigation channel was accomplished by employing the idle labour during the slack season. "The traditional land hunger of the individual peasant family is enlisted for a collective effort to create more land for the whole community." This happens because the team controls land, the additional benefits to the team are visible and the members of the team supplying extra labour earn extra workpoints (Robinson, 1966g, 71). Once again the question of work motivation and incentive is mixed up by her. It is not the traditional land hunger or additional benefits (which are not necessarily visible) but the fear of a reduced share in the division of total team income resulting from non-participation that makes members come forward for collective labour. Participation adds to workpoints, but not necessarily to individual income. Thus, "as long as there are some members in a team taking the lead, the odds are that others will follow" (Liu Minquan, 1989, 25).

Dumonr (1966, 101) held the view that the Great Leap was the Chinese way to emerge out of the vicious circle of underdevelopment. However, the mistakes were not corrected in time, raising the cost of correction later. Macfarquhar (1983, 333) also thinks that through the Leap Mao "hammered home" the point that in underdeveloped economies, "it is critical that the people should be seized of the idea that they do not have to sit submissively under the yoke of nature". He concludes: "But the excesses of the Leap and its ultimate collapse could have stunned a less resilient people into apathy about economic development." Joan Robinson, besides approving the Leap in principle, thought that rational corrections were introduced well in time: "The Great Leap Forward in China in 1958, the set-back that followed and the recovery now accomplished form one of the most dramatic episodes in economic history that this dramatic age has seen" (Robinson, 1966g, 69). This is true, with the difference that the script was written by the rightists. During this drama Mao, as Robinson claimed later, "represented the opposition" (Robinson, 1969a, 82).

Joan Robinson did not accept the commonly held view of the post-Leap developments as a retreat. There was a retreat in regard to birth control, as she herself admitted. The campaign could not be resumed before 1963. She also admitted that "substitution of labour for capital did not work out" in the case of steel (Robinson, 1966e, 548).Commenting on Chen (1964), she stated: "Chen leaves the impression of a retreat from the principles of the Great Leap, while later visitors report that the reorganisation represented the ascendancy of common sense over enthusiasm and that the commune system, though flexible, is by no means disorganised" (Robinson, 1966e, 547).

Until the cultural revolution, Joan Robinson continued to project the rational manner in which the Chinese managed the disasters of the Leap, justifying on occasions her own back-tracking on a number of issues. She had, as noted earlier, believed that the socialisation of agriculture in China would be gradual and not a steamroller, as it was in the Soviet Union. However, before she could fully explain the high tide of cooperativisation, Mao moved at supersonic speed to collapse about 75,000 cooperatives into just 26,425 communes: an average of 28 cooperatives per commune.[10] Yet collectivisation was described as "a gradual process". In the case of peasants, the factor in "inclining them to accept co-operation" was a holding size too small "to build a family fortune on". The rich peasants had to accept cooperation because they "could not find hands to employ" due to the peasantisation of the landless after the land reform. Considering that the role played by private plots was larger than their size and the deteriorating food situation in 1956, the argument is not very convincing. The main factor in high-speed coopertivisation was mentioned, however, only in passing: "party members, soldiers returning from the revolutionary war and those who had become convinced of the benefits of co-operation could persuade their neighbours." There was never any attempt to explain why communes had suddenly become so necessary, except for giving the impression that the process of collectivisation was spread over eight years:

> In the course of eight years the countryside was carried through several stages of collectivization, till the communes were formed in the Great Leap in 1958. In the uprush of enthusiasm, in some places the movement was carried to extremes. (This did not happen everywhere). (Robinson, 1968e, 684–5)

Not only that she never offered any convincing explanation for the mad rush towards collectivisation,[11] Joan Robinson also changed her views on the role of collectivisation in the Chinese development. On earlier view, the collective had few inherent advantages over smaller scales of operation in the absence of mechanisation. Collectivisation was necessary to reap the benefits of mechanisation, which included a higher rate of agricultural surplus for industry on the one hand and the release of surplus labour on the other. In short, collectivisation was to perform the same extractive function as in the Soviet Union, but hopefully not as heartlessly. On a net basis, no transfer of resources out of agriculture took place in China under Mao.[12]

Campaigning for the Maoist Point of View

The withdrawal of Soviet aid in July 1960 was a major event that worked on Joan Robinson to change some of her set views on the Chinese development. The withdrawal was sudden, carried out with military speed, leaving the Chinese bewildered. The "much malicious misrepresentation of China in the Western press, now being repeated and exaggerated in Russia" (Robinson, 1964h, vii), led her to take on the job of explaining "the Chinese point of view" in terms not very different from dependency-style arguments[13]:

> To them it seems clear that the only way of escape for the hungry and miserable is first to assert their national independence and then to build up economic independence. They will soon find that, to this end, socialism is the only way. Anti-imperialism, anti-neo-colonialism and anti-capitalism are various aspects of the same thing. (Robinson, 1964f, 234)

The first departure from the Soviet economic doctrines made by the Chinese was in regard to collectivisation. In the Soviet Union, collectivisation had been a means to mechanisation. With effect from 1956, the Chinese turned it into a substitute for mechanisation: "[S]ince it would be a long time before equipment would be available, the only hope of improving productivity lay in mobilising labour" (Robinson, 1964b, 199). Second, Joan Robinson discounted the significance of private plots in the Chinese agricultural economy: it was relatively more important in the Soviet Union. Reviewing Walker (1965) she noted his observation "that the area actually given out for private plots has always been much less than the law allows". This suggested to "her that the peasants were not so keen on them as (by analogy with the U.S.S.R.) is usually supposed" (Robinson, 1966a, 159). Third, in 1959 the Chinese began to view the marketed surplus of agriculture as the crucial limit on industrial development, something antithetical to "the dogma, learned from the Russians, that the first law of socialist development is the permanent priority of heavy industry". By 1962, the strategy in China was: agriculture the foundation and industry the leading sector.[14] This shift, according to Robinson, was reflected in the strategy of planning as follows[15]:

> The proportion of state investment allotted to agriculture was stepped up; industrial investment was deflected towards the needs of agriculture—tractors, farm machinery, fertilisers; for scarce consumer goods the country is given an advantage over the town. In 1963, as things grew a little easier, the Party watchword was: It is not yet time to relax. The policy is to increase output and to draw off surplus smoothly without having to turn the screw on the peasants. (Robinson, 1964e, 291, 296)

Obviously, she had changed her views on the role of heavy industry as well. She had clearly been in favour of a priority for heavy industry in socialist development as a key to chasing a high rate of capital accumulation. As she suggested to Adler:

> Under socialism, planning presupposes a fair degree of ability to foresee the future en gross, so that the expansion of the aggregate market as distinct from particular and individual markets can be rationally allowed for, and it is a comparatively easy matter to use the products of heavy industry with efficiency and advantage. (Adler, 1957, 63)

A reverberation of this earlier emphasis on steel can also be seen in the following statement made some time later:

> Western critics nowadays often suggest that the emphasis on steel in China (and in India) was a misguided application of Soviet dogma to a situation which it did not fit. Certainly a switch of emphasis to agriculture in 1960 was necessary (and would have been advantageous in India) but however tough the first stage of industrialisation may be, it is hard to see how it could lead forward without a basis in steel. (Robinson, 1966e, 548)

During her fourth visit in October 1964, Joan Robinson came to the conclusion that the Soviet withdrawal had led to the development of technologies appropriate to the Chinese conditions. If she had any doubts about the efficiency of a strategy of self-reliance, they were dispelled by her visit to North Korea.[16]

In applauding China's departures from what she described as Soviet doctrines, Joan Robinson was not merely appreciating the adaptations made necessary by different objective data. After her third visit, she seemed well-briefed by the Chinese on the Sino-Soviet ideological rift.[17] Like many others, she had become critical of the Soviet Union after the world came to know of Stalin's atrocities. However, until after the third visit to China, there is no trace of an anti-Soviet stance. Indeed some of her writings could be described as unduly favourable to the Soviet Union.[18] East-West trade in general and Soviet-British trade in particular, together with the underlying theme of peaceful co-existence, were subjects which continued to occupy her attention.[19] She thought that despite Soviet economic errors, Westerners "have more to learn than teach" (Robinson, 1964m, 493).

Her first visit to China was a direct outcome of the deliberations at the Moscow economic conference. *The Times* had talked of an unofficial business delegation to China, of which Joan Robinson was the only non-business member, as "organised under the auspices of trading organisations set up after the Moscow economic conference".[20] This organisation was named as the British Council for the Promotion of International Trade (BCPI). Joan Robinson was its vice chairman. The BCPI was condemned as "a Communist front organisation".[21] She had strongly protested against these "vague insinuations" (Robinson, 1953d, e). It was at the invitation of the Chinese counterpart of the BCPI that she paid her first three trips to China. Denominated as the China Committee for the Promotion of International Trade (CCPIT), it was headed by Chi chao-ting, a Chicago-trained economic historian with whom Joan Robinson made friends at the Moscow economic conference.[22]

At the Moscow conference, Joan Robinson noted that "Russians, Chinese and English understand each other's style—reserve, understatement, commonsense". She discovered in it an "Entente of Tea Drinkers" (Robinson, 1952b, 11). The entente seems to have ended by her third visit to China. The Russians were unreservedly attacking the Chinese position. The China of the Leap could not be accused of much common sense. As for the English, Joan Robinson's defence of China and its policies had become anything but an understatement.

Joan Robinson has not been known as a political activist.[23] However, after the third visit and mainly because of the ideological conflict between the Soviet Union and China, she became an active campaigner for the Chinese cause. Before she knew of the two-line struggle within China, she had cast her vote for the Maoist line in the international communist movement. The China Policy Study Group (CPSG) was set up in 1963, which started to publish the *Broadsheet* from January 1964. Recognising in the first issue that the Sino-Soviet "differences embody two major concepts of how the world is to move from its present state of inequality and poverty, oppression and war, to a society of peace and economic and social emancipation", it declared that its aim "will be to summarise Chinese views".[24] In the third issue, Joan Robinson's name appeared among the sponsors.[25] In this context, it is not hard to understand Joan Robinson's sympathetic statement of "the Chinese point of view" on the Sino-Soviet[26] ideological rift, Sino-Indian border conflict, Tibet and even the bomb (Robinson, 1964i).[27]

Before the Sino-Soviet ideological rift, those favouring friendship with China worked under the aegis of the Britain-China Friendship Association. After the rift, supporters of the Chinese line broke away in May 1965 to form the SACU—Society for Anglo-Chinese Understanding. Its main organ was *SACU News*, which became *China Now* in May 1970. Joseph Needham, the renowned Cambridge historian of science and civilisation in China, was its chairman and Joan Robinson the deputy chairman. SACU was designed to be non-political, but its aim essentially was "to make known the Chinese point of view on all kinds of matters".[28] The obituary published by SACU brought out quite clearly the active role played by Joan Robinson:

> With the onset of the Sino-Soviet Polemic, heavy clamps were put on the activities of the C.P. controlled [British-] China Friendship Assoc[iation]—to discuss China's foreign policy or the people's communes would offend the Soviet Union and was therefore, taboo. Joan Robinson and others were

> quick to see the absurdity of this situation and she with Joseph Needham and George Thomson[29] set out to work to create a new body on a much broader basis. Having first interested a dozen or so fellow academics, they issued an appeal for support for the infant organisation. (*SACU Newsletter*, September 1983, 1)

As information became more widely available in the post-Mao China, the periodicals claiming to represent the Chinese point of view withered away. The *Broadsheet* was not published after May 1982, with the closing admission that the criticism of being "a mere echo of Chinese official policy [was) the more serious and that it was often justified".[30] SACU witnessed a "great debate" of its own at the start of the eighties.[31] *Eastern Horizon* from Hong Kong also carried many of Joan Robinson's writings on China. Its last issue appeared in September 1981. A letter from the editor contained in the August 1981 issue plainly stated that the magazine "was born at a time when the outside world had little access to news or reports about developments in China, particularly on the positive side of such developments. This was the gap we attempted to close."

Joan Robinson insisted that she "was not interested in discussing ideology", ironically in an article presenting the Chinese view and at a time when she had taken an anti-Soviet position. All ideologies, including Marxist ideology, were nothing more than rationalisations which appealed "to high metaphysical principles to justify policies that arise out of mundane necessity". Revisionism, the Chinese label for the Soviet approach, was seen by her as belonging to the realm of theology, where to prove that "a statement is heretical is more damaging than to prove that it is false". Having said that, she pleaded that shorn of "the ideological style in public pronouncements", the Chinese possessed an "empirical, commonsense outlook" (Robinson, 1964f, 232–3). In general a vehement opponent of theological arguments, obscurantist styles and metaphysical approaches,[32] she was not very clear when it came to applying the same tests to the Chinese. While conceding that the "controversy between *One divides into two* (correct) and *Two combine into one* (heretical)"[33] was being conducted "in the theological style, when points are scored by striking analogies and apposite quotations from the Fathers, rather than in the scientific style, which relies upon controlled experiment", she hastened to add: "But theology is necessary when doctrines are derived from the written word, to expound the texts and to adapt them to new problems." She did not think that "the argument—more properly it should be called an exercise"—would lead to any purge, as believed in the Western press. "Up to date, the chief heretic is still in his job, and still defending his opinion" (Robinson, 1965c, 12).

Slogans such as "putting politics in command" upset even some sympathetic visitors like Dumonr (1966). However, Joan Robinson was ready to interpret it as "taking a long-term rather than a short-term view of economic policy for instance that it is worthwhile to plant trees on the hillside to check erosion". And in situations where the same slogan caused economic losses, as in the case of close planting, she observed the practice to be "contrary to the spirit of Mao's teaching, which requires that all generalisations should be adapted to the specific situation in each locality". Second, it meant "that the peasants must not be alienated, as happened in USSR, but brought to understand what they are being asked to do". Third, it encouraged democracy: "There is no better example of democracy at the grass roots than the question of settling the value of work points" (Robinson, 1966g, 70–1).

Joan Robinson's assessment of the Leap and its aftermath was not based on full knowledge. According to her, overenthusiasm led to some mistakes that were corrected in time and in the spirit of experimental method, especially those in regard to the communes. In the light of what is known now, it appears that she was no less enthusiastic in supporting views, prescriptions and operational details provided by enthusiasts of the Maoist line.

Her visits in 1963 and 1964 coincided with "*the all-round turn for the better* [Italics in original] in the economy".[34] She was not there during the disastrous years following the Leap. Those were the days when politics was put in command and, far from being Joan Robinson's long-term view of economic policy, the slogan promoted ill-assorted, misconceived and obviously unpractical policies—the existence of all of which she recognised but the extent of the damage admitted was never more than the official Chinese story. First, the enlargement of the unit of account to the level of the commune had no economic justification, and her earlier writings had clearly raised the issue of the economic size of cooperatives in the absence of mechanisation. Second, the abandonment of payments according to work in favour of payments according to need suggested a short-sighted view of the economy, while the concept of communal eating and the attack on the family represented a complete disregard of the sentiments of the masses. Third, the elimination of whatever was left of the market and private ownership—private plots, household possessions and sideline activities—denied the economy the flexible points whose role as small cushions becomes clear only during economic storms that a myopic state cannot weather.

She agreed with the Maoist view that natural disasters and the suddenness of the Soviet withdrawal, and not the policy mistakes, were mainly responsible for the worst economic performance. However, the mistakes were no less serious and their correction was guided not by Mao's thought, but by the realism of the "right deviationists"—Peng Dehuai, for instance, who argued that putting politics in command was no substitute for concrete economic measures. If after her 1963 and 1964 visits Joan Robinson was able to tell the world about a flexible three-decker commune system with the team[35] as the basic unit of account, the end of the public canteens, rewards commensurate with work, rural fairs as part of the three-level marketing, agriculture the foundation, price stability and an unequivocal support for population control—in short about "the all-round turn for the better in the economy"—it was because the "right deviationists" led by "the chief heretic" and abetted by the pragmatist Chou En-lai had succeeded in putting in command a strict economic adjustment programme.[36]

As the turnaround in the economy became visible, and the re-attainment of pre-Leap levels of key outputs seemed within reach, the Chinese were once again debating the basic question that Joan Robinson had raised in her lectures in China in 1957—how best to run the economy. At that time she had suggested that the moral method could only be a supplement, and not a system by itself like the market mechanism running itself or a planning organisation managed by bureaucracy. Going against the essence of the Soviet economic reform, that is, decentralised enterprises, Mao attempted a political decentralisation option by putting politics in command through the communes. He was defeated by harsh economic realities, the adverse impact of which could only be reversed by a strong dose of centralised discipline, mixed with a regulated role for the market and monetary incentives.

Joan Robinson praised these achievements in China, but worried about "a reproduction of managerial capitalism" in Eastern Europe. According to her, monetary incentives are not only "a denial of the moral content of socialism [but] dangerous also from a purely economic point of view". Under capitalism, the money motive had led to money income rising faster than average output, leading to a chronic inflationary condition. "Chairman Mao launched the Cultural Revolution to forestall these developments in China." The "right deviationists" were now dubbed as the "capitalist roaders" and the slogan of "putting politics in command" was reinterpreted as "serve the people" ideology (Robinson, 1967g, 46–50, h, 41–2[37]).

Translated into simple economics, adherence to this ethic had the microeconomic effect of de-linking productivity growth from wage increases and the macroeconomic effect of a strong incomes policy. In addition, the Chinese had also been able to keep the growth of aggregate demand below that of the supply. These, in the eyes of Joan Robinson, were the "two reasons why Chinese were able to avoid inflation".[38] By implication, the Chinese should also have avoided the struggle under capitalism during inflation whereby "everyone has to fight to maintain his share, and when the total to be shared is not expanding, the fight grows bitter indeed" (Robinson, 1974h, 488). An implication of the analysis by Liu Minquan (1989) is that this is not the case. In situations where the shareable total was not expanding, commune members had to work on collective projects to maintain the value of their workpoints and thus to protect the already low threshold incomes.

As was noted earlier, the fundamental point that Joan Robinson made about economic reform in Eastern Europe[39] was that it did not tackle the main problem and the one these economies shared with the capitalist economies: the centralised planned economies and the decentralised capitalist economies both left the initiative with the producer. Consumer sovereignty in the West was a myth; tastes were managed through the media. In the East, there existed an anti-consumption bias.

Decentralisation towards the enterprises, whether by using the profit criterion as an index of efficiency or an autonomous price policy, still left the consumers high and dry. In China, the internal trade ministry stood between the producers and the consumers, acting in the interest of the latter while placing wholesale orders for the retailers. It appears that in Robinson's view this ministry played in China's development a role no less significant than that of the external trade ministry in the Japanese development. She stated in no uncertain terms that such a class of functionaries "can operate, however, only in the setting of civic morality that prevails in China" (Robinson, 1967g, 49).

More burden was now placed on moral incentives for growth as well as stability, leaving little role for economic policy. How was the serve-the-people ideology of the internal trade ministry (incidentally created by the rightists to deal with the capitalists in the early days of the People's Republic) different from serve-the-people ideology of enterprises themselves? Questions like this were not asked. Soon Robinson would see a lot of order in the chaos of the cultural revolution.[40] The stage for this had been set by her increasingly sympathetic concern to present whatever was the Chinese point of view, or more correctly, the Maoist view. At the second general meeting of SACU, held against the background of the cultural revolution, Needham emphasised the need to change the non-political character of the organisation and "to adopt a more resolute stand" on matters like the cultural revolution, "which had been totally misunderstood".[41] SACU had also to respond to the CP-dominated Britain-China Friendship Association (BCFA) which "passed day to day resolutions on political matters". A resolution was moved, which, among other things, stated:

> The conclusions that members reach are their own, without attempts at mutual censorship. Similarly, speakers on SACU platforms and writers in SACU publications are expressing their own individual points of view, but these should *necessarily* [Emphasis added] be compatible with the stated aims of SACU and therefore conducive to understanding.

Joan Robinson had argued against a similar resolution in the first annual general meeting, which was defeated. Now she supported the above resolution, which "was enthusiastically carried". To her "it was quite clear that SACU now found itself in a 'difficult and prickly situation' and the earlier objections to the resolution no longer held as far as she was concerned" (*SACU News*, June 1967, 1). The council of management adopted a policy statement, expressing its total commitment to the cultural revolution and Mao's thought.[42]

Thus, Joan Robinson was committed to the cultural revolution before embarking on her fifth visit—"short visit (though an intensive one) to China to study the Cultural Revolution" (Robinson, 1968b, 1). She had expressed some interest in moral incentives since the second visit. After the third visit she even declared that "[e]conomic development is a moral problem". This was, however, said in a context. Looking at China's prospects in a longer-term perspective, she forecast major strides in economy, society and culture despite an expected addition of 200 million to the adult population if "the present trend of development in China rolls smoothly on for the next twenty years". In 1964, the allusion could only have been to the development strategy implemented by the capitalist roaders. Among "the necessary conditions for all this to be realised" were included external peace, the consequent hope that China was not "obliged to enter the nuclear arms race" and that the party continued "rectifying" itself "to keep its virtue". This was the time of "socialist education" and "four clean-ups". The economics as well as politics of the time met with her approval. But she still wondered: "Can human nature bear the strain of such high standards for another twenty years and more?" She was already seeing some signs of strain:

> The time of frugality, hard work, and a slow rise in comfort from the bottom upwards will not be over in twenty years (it could be over in a decade if the population had not been rising and if luxury and wangling crept in at the top, sulkiness at the bottom would soon let the economy drift into stagnation). Economic development is a moral problem. (Robinson, 1964g, 756)

However, when this "wangling crept in at the top" led to rumours in the West about a purge in the party, she saw during her fourth visit that "the chief heretic is still in his job, and still defending his opinion". She now clearly admitted the existence of another strand of thought in China. At a time when Khrushchev had fallen, improving the prospects of external peace, she was justifying "the trouble and expense to test a bomb" and musing over a "strange world where one more bomb is a hopeful sign of peace". In less than a decade, the Nixon visit to China following Kissinger's secret flight through Pakistan would further secure external peace. But it was the cultural revolution disturbing China's internal peace that caught her imagination at that stage; a magnification of her view of economic development as a moral problem.

The Cultural Revolution: Illusion of a Cooperative Solution

Joan Robinson had rejected the competitive system for its inherent inequity, resulting from abolishing the moral problem by denying the conflict between self-interest and altruism. She noted with satisfaction that the May uprising of radical students in France could not be deflected by the Communist Party and trade unions to the ordinary wage demands. The students wanted to change the system, and not to be co-opted by it.[43] The planning system, first criticised for its bureaucratic tendency, was also now believed prone to inequity as, among other things, "a sad consequence of the achievement of universal education and equality of opportunity, which the Chinese aim to avoid" (Robinson, 1969a, 151). The differentials caused by intellectual property were considered no less serious than those arising from the existence of private property. The search was on for a cooperative system.[44] Joan Robinson intervened in the debate on the modelling of producer cooperatives. Domar (1966) modelled Soviet collective farm as a producer cooperative. A group of workers are assigned a given amount of land, and they are to share the net produce. In Domar's framework, their objective function would be to maximise return per unit of work. According to Joan Robinson, the more natural thing to do would be to maximise income per man-year. She also criticised the seminal model by Ward (1958), in which the number of workers to be employed could be varied. She argued that a cooperative cannot be assumed to dismiss workers to gain income increments. "In setting up models of this type it is necessary to begin by asking the elementary economic question *cui bono*"[45] (Robinson, 1967b, 222–3).

For the conditions under which an egalitarian cooperative system would work, she looked towards the experiment in China under cultural revolution rather than providing a theoretical framework of her own.[46] The slogan "Serve the people" seemed to answer "the elementary economic question *cui bono*?"[47] It implied, "Industrial discipline is based not upon individual incentives but upon the appeal to everyone to contribute what he can." A socialist revolution aims "to exalt the humble and meek, to put down the mighty". Once this has happened, the humble "have a way of becoming mighty in their turn. The aim of the Cultural Revolution now going on in China is to check this tendency and keep alive the spirit of service" (Robinson, 1968e, 689–90). In short, the message was altruism not egoism, interest of the people rather than self-interest and moral rather than material incentives.

The principles and policies which during the Leap were considered hasty and extreme constituted the hard core of the cultural revolution. The correctives and readjustments introduced at the behest of the rightists led by Liu were praised: "[A] lot of nonsense was wrung out and highly practical form of organisation was ordered" (Robinson, 1968e, 685–9). During the cultural revolution, when this wringing-out of nonsense was declared to be a capitalist road, she just went along. As the abandoned ideas of the Leap were brought back with a much more militant ideology, Joan Robinson believed the moment had arrived for the ideas which were ahead of the time during the Leap (Robinson, 1968b, 3). Thus, her writings contain two stories, one relating to the abandoned extremism of the Leap now found practical and the other describing the practical ideas of the Leap as an NEP which had outlived its utility.

According to the first story, the discontinuation of private plots, food distribution according to need and even the backyard steelmaking now made sense:

> [In the] famous Tachai brigade which is held up as an example … private plots have been abolished. Another interesting thing is that in the Great Leap the idea was introduced of distributing food according to need, instead of according to work points earned. They have just now introduced it in Tachai … So they are just beginning to put into practice some of the extreme ideas of the Great Leap which were at that time premature …

> The Great Leap was a large scale example of [the trial and error] principle. It contained great errors, yet the enormous investments that were made in that period, now yielding returns, could hardly have been made in any other way. Even the back-yard steel, generally considered in the West as mere nonsense, left behind an important benefit in breaking down the inferiority complex of the peasants in respect of industrial workers. (Robinson, 1968e, 690)

Dazhai [Tachai], according to her, was a kind of pilot project for the cultural revolution. The trial and error had been reduced to a smaller scale, to that of a brigade. Despite conceding the fact that "these achievements were due to personal leadership", Robinson thought "the example can be reduced to a system once it has been pioneered". She also believed that the Dazhai system would help overcome the problem of inequality between the communes. This of course was an important element in the cooperative system for which she looked towards China. She maintained:

> There are very great differences in the level of income per head that is obtainable in different communes for reasons of geography. This gives rise to 'socialist rent'. Moreover it sets up a cumulative movement. Land tax is negligible for an area where output has been rising, as it was fixed on the basis of yields at the time of land reform. A rich commune saves and invests in land improvements and in installing small-scale industry, while a poor one struggles to feed its members. It would be politically dangerous to penalise the prosperous commune, and economically extravagant to deflect investment to the poor one. The Dazhai example appeals to the poor commune to pull itself up by its own bootstraps, offers rewards in pride and honour that (once food and shelter are secure) may be preferred to anything that money could buy. Thus apparently starry-eyed idealism is found once more to be based on solid Chinese commonsense. (Robinson, 1968b, 3–4)

It was starry-eyed idealism, at best. A comprehensive analysis of inter-commune inequality shows it to be an extremely serious and tricky problem (Nolan, 1983c). Measures like the self-reliance approach of Dazhai were hardly the serious policy response required for the purpose (Nolan, 1988, 76–7). If anything, a strategy of self-reliance by communes would only aggravate the problem by leaving the rich communes free to get richer and richer.

Now consider the NEP story. The capitalist roaders were those elements in the party who were following "the Chinese Khrushchev" Liu Shao-chi. During the reverses of the Leap, the group was involved in reorganising the economy to adjust to the three bad years. Among the more important measures taken were the team as the accounting unit for distributing income and deploying labour, local fairs as outlets for household output, redirection of investment towards agriculture and a steady supply of consumer goods

> so as to induce the peasants to want to earn money. This might be regarded as a kind of NEP; but Lenin intended the NEP as a temporary device in face of difficulties, which was to be reversed as soon as they were overcome. The rightists in China advocated these measures as permanent and wanted to push them further. Recovery, starting from 1962, and the fruits of the huge investments made in 1958, began to show that the Great Leap was not a failure after all, but the rightists were reluctant to admit it. (Robinson, 1968b, 2–3)

During her first visit in 1953, she maintained that the NEP cap did not fit the concessions given to the capitalists in the early years of the revolution. Soviet NEP was "a step back from an over-hasty rush towards socialism" while the Chinese package was designed "to lead smoothly into socialism" (Robinson, 1954a, 7). Now during the fifth visit she was informed in November 1967 by the cultural revolutionaries in Shanghai that the Chinese package was the first attack by the rightists, and that the "five-antis" campaign was what she had thought it was not: a "root-and-branch" campaign against capitalism. According to the cultural revolutionaries cited by Joan Robinson, the rightist influence increased again in 1957 as they used whatever political power they still had and "the prestige of intellectuals, who were still irreplaceable in administration and the educational system". To this the party had responded by the anti-rightist movement of 1957. The worst attack, she was told, came in the three bitter years of 1959–61. As she noted: "Party persons in authority were responsible rather than the old bourgeoisie", who stood for "restoration [which] means revisionism on the Khrushchev model—the use of economic incentives, encouragement of private trade and so forth". Liu Shao-chi, Deng Xio-ping and Po I-po were identified as the leaders of the capitalist road (Robinson, 1969a, 47, 53, 140). With help from *Peking Review*,[48] Liu's views were further elaborated as follows:

> "The Right deviation in 1962" refers to the period when the three bad years of harvest failures were over, but Liu Shao-chi was taking advantage of that experience to press for the economic ideas that he believed in particularly the development of individualistic monetary incentives in agricultural production at the expense of the principles of cooperation and collective responsibility that Mao upheld. Liu advocated the extension of plots for private use, the extension of the rural fairs at which individual households could sell their products in conditions of a free market, the increase in the number of small enterprises in the villages run on the principle of private profit, and the fixing of output quotas in the annual production plan on the basis of households instead of on the basis of teams or brigades. (Robinson, 1969a, 81–2)

The "dress rehearsal" for the cultural revolution started with the "four clean-ups" in 1964. Local fairs were discontinued and the household products turned over to marketing cooperatives and state trading. During this campaign, the struggle at Dazhai provided a preview of the cultural revolution (Robinson, 1968b, 3). While discussing the "wrong tendency of 1964 which was 'Left' in form but Right in essence", she observed:

> Mao Tse-tung in one sense represented the opposition at this time, and Liu the government. He had evidently been in a weak position during the bad years that followed the Great Leap of 1958. It was officially admitted that the disastrous harvest failures were not only due to the formidable weather conditions of those years but were partly due to mistakes in the Party's work—political mistakes, such as forcing the pace in setting up the communes, and technical mistakes such as the indiscriminate application of rules, for instance, deep ploughing and close planting, without considering the variations in local conditions. Mao's adversaries played up the mistakes. At this time the Rightists 'came to their high tide'. (Robinson, 1969a, 82–3)

In a review of Karol (1975, 112–4), who doubted the claim made in the above quotation about the weakening of Mao's influence, Joan Robinson reiterated her position, saying that "Mao himself complained that he was then being treated like the ancestor at a funeral, who is revered but not obeyed" (Robinson, 1975i, 217). But Mao also said things, noted by Caute, which make nonsense of *The Cultural Revolution* by her. Caute states:

> Certainly one would not gather from Professor Robinson's pages that life in China at this time was as Mao subsequently described it to Edgar Snow: 'Later the conflict during the Cultural Revolution developed into a war between two factions—first with spears, then mortars ... When foreigners reported that China was in great chaos, they were not telling lies. It had been true'. (Caute, 1977, 377)

However, after Mao had stated the above,[49] Joan Robinson also fell in line: "The conception of the Cultural Revolution was evidently to let the pot boil and to see what would come to the top, but when factions of Red Guards began actually to shoot at each other with stolen rifles, a halt was called" (Robinson, 1972b, 321).

Just as she had neglected to state the Soviet case while informing the world about the Chinese point of view (Robinson, 1964f), she did not do justice to the viewpoint of the "Chinese Khrushchev" and his fellow "capitalist roaders", admitted to be "not merely scoundrels" but having "a point of view", though it had to "be glimpsed between the lines of the accusations made against them". In the first place, the Leap was a misadventure "for which a heavy price was paid in three bad years that followed". Parenthetically, she observed that the "rightists refused to recognise the return in increased production later enjoyed on the great investments which threw the economy off balance while they were being made". Nor did they "acknowledge that the communes have been vindicated by the continuous increase in harvests since 1962". Second, the rightists stood for organisation and authority, a top-down chain of command and the desirability of "a more comfortable standard of life" for those higher up in the hierarchy. What is required of the workers is "obedience and diligence" and not "their heads full of political wind".[50] Third, the rightists wanted to force the pace of industrialisation by building a corps of managers fast enough by drawing "upon the old lettered class, even if they were landlords and reactionaries in the past",[51] rather than "wait till the mass of the population are educated". To this group, which Robinson was told was "preparing to take power",[52] was attributed the Russian disease of foisting "a capitalist superstructure ... on a socialist base [which] inevitably tends to erode a socialist base". This is because, according to Mao, "*[i]deas may become a material force*" [emphasis in original]. To counter this, the first line of attack was provided by the Red Guards,[53] "*the lucky children* [emphasis in original] who take New China for granted". Having "been plunged into revolution ... they learned more about socialism and about China in a few weeks than they could ever have learned from reading pious stories at home". The real struggle, however, had to be waged by the industrial workers. The rightists, she wrote, attempted to buy them off through "what is not very happily called *economism*—paying bonus wages and promoting apprentices to full pay" [emphasis in original]. The qualifier "not very happily" was appropriate because the argument ran counter to her view of consumer sovereignty under Chinese socialism. However, once again she saw a practical side to the Chinese ideology to conclude: "All this may sound idealistic or even sentimental, but it has a very practical advantage. China still has long years of toil and accumulation of resources lying ahead before she can establish an unassailable position as a great modem nation. High morale is much more economical than incentive wages" (Robinson, 1968c, 214–22). Incentive wages were considered as inimical to socialism as the profit motive. She could see the "important difference between using profits as a criterion of success in an enterprise and relying on profits as a motive for activity; but the Chinese maintain that the first will inevitably lead to the second" (Robinson, 1969a, 12–3).

The picture that emerges here of the capitalist roaders or the rightists is one of economic disciplinarians. Yet they were accused of anarchism, which in the case of Liu surprised even Joan Robinson: "At the same time that he is attacked and mocked for advocating slavish obedience to authority and maintaining that Party discipline requires commands to be carried out even when they are wrong, he is also accused of the opposite vice." She could see that Liu was being quoted out of context, but she fudged the issue as follows:

> The quotation[[54]] is not intended as a contribution to historical analysis[[55]]. It is evidently provided to strengthen the hand of the moderate and sensible group in any organization in their arguments with a colleague who is carrying the injunction to defend his own opinions to unreasonable lengths. (Robinson, 1969a, 148–9)

Liu had argued that exploitation was necessary for development, something Joan Robinson could also be accused of.[56] A clarification was, therefore, necessary:

> They are digging up a lot of things from Liu Shao-chi's past now and presenting him to the people as having been always a bad man, always thinking of installing capitalism. It seems to me that that was not the case. In any group there is bound to be a right wing and a left wing, and Liu Shao-chi represented the cautious approach to development—and the pro-Russian line. One of the sayings that is always quoted against him is that 'exploitation is a good thing'. This is regarded with the utmost horror. What he meant was that China is at a very low level of development and it is better to let capitalism raise it a bit before you go over to socialism. That is to say, let the capitalists expand and employ labour. It seems to me that he was perhaps too cautious and conservative, not trusting the people in the way Mao did. (Robinson, 1968e, 692–3)

This left no doubt as to the side Joan Robinson had chosen during the cultural revolution. The post-Leap recovery package was an NEP, which had done its job, and not a long-term development strategy.

Joan Robinson disputed the suggestions that "there was a collapse of the economy and a danger of total disintegration during the turmoil that the Cultural Revolution produced". According to her, "For the most part this was not allowed to interfere with production, but sometimes it did." In fact, "the great release of energy", together with "the possibilities of cutting out red-tape and reducing the ratio of administrative personnel to productive workers, led to such high rates of output that many enterprises overtook arrears and fulfilled their planned assignments for the year two or three months ahead of schedule". No figures were given. In Shanghai, the main industrial centre, output in 1967 was expected to be lower than in the preceding year due to the trouble at coal mines, but "a Great Leap" was predicted for 1968. In a number of industries, technical advances and cost savings due to organisational simplification were reported. Western businessmen attending the Canton trade fair were said to have reported business as usual. "Agriculture, which matters far more, appears in an excellent shape." The year 1967, "the sixth good year in succession", was "said to be the largest in recorded history". The following year was also stated to have yielded a good harvest. Despite the population having touched the 700-million mark, "the general impression seems to be that both consumption per head and the accumulation of stocks of grain are steadily rising" (Robinson, 1968b, 3, 1969a, 149).

The macroeconomic reason for the economy to keep going, according to Joan Robinson, is that the discredited high rate of investment was now yielding dividends. Mao's high-speed strategy was after all not wrong. Just as the Leap enthusiasm had put a ratchet behind the rate of investment, the popular energy released by the cultural revolution was now maintaining a high growth of output as well as investment. However, a high investment rate is not necessarily the guarantee for good economic growth. At that stage of Chinese development, a high rate of investment was part of the problem, not solution.[57] With extreme fluctuations of policy, all that is possible to say is that the state of the economy in the cultural revolution was not as bad as in the Leap years. And the stabilising elements for this had been instituted by those condemned as the capitalist roaders.

In industrial management, the contribution of the cultural revolution was to avoid "the emergence of a managerial elite or meritocrats" (Robinson, 1968h, 5). A "high degree of devolution and workers' self-management was established". Politics was put in command of the management of enterprise, but the essential concern of the new management remained production as distinct from its Yugoslav counterpart, which controlled prices as well as products, and the Soviet bloc enterprises, which were asked to show profits. "Prices and supplies are given to an enterprise in China" (Robinson, 1969a, 132–4). Now this system of maximising production, given the prices, inputs and product-mix, was devised by the capitalist roaders. The difference made by the cultural revolution was "that pride rather than money earnings gives the incentive to the workers and management alike to maintain and improve production" (*ibid.*, 133). Whether it actually made a difference to output growth is another matter.

In agriculture, the economic core of the commune re-organisation carried out by the capitalist roaders remained intact. The most crucial element in it was the scaling-down of the accounting unit from the unwieldy commune to the more manageable team. During the Leap, and even later, Joan Robinson described it as a tribute to the Chinese sense of the practical. The measure was introduced by the capitalist roaders. The cultural revolution had no effect on this measure, conceptually based on the recognition of material incentives. In Joan Robinson's own words written after the cultural revolution: "In a large co-operative the relation between an individual's efforts and his share in the reward is too much diluted." That is why the communes were reorganised to give a smaller unit—the team—more importance (Robinson, 1968e, 685–6). Again, "Chinese policy and political education lay great stress on the moral factor in economic life but they are not starry eyed. They do not rely on moral incentives alone to evoke the heavy toil that a still primitive agriculture needs" (Robinson, 1972b, 132).

Although the idea of "agriculture is the foundation and industry the leading factor" was part of the "Ten Great Relationships" announced by Mao in 1956, a concrete effort to ensure proper agricultural-industrial interaction did not start until the rightist seized the initiative to put together their reform package in the post-Leap years. As was noted by Joan Robinson:

> During the bad years the Chinese planners realized that they had not sufficiently freed themselves from the Soviet example. They increased investment in industrial products directly useful to agriculture, such as fertilisers and machinery, and they increased supplies of consumer goods to the villages so that team members would be keen to earn money and therefore willing to sell their produce. At this time the slogan was adopted—agriculture is the foundation and industry the leading factor. (Robinson, 1968e, 686)

At another place, she stated:

> In the early years after the Revolution there wasn't anything to buy in the Soviet Union, so the villagers had no motive for wanting to sell their crops to get money to buy goods from industry. But in China industry was instructed to produce goods that the villagers would want to buy—bicycles, radio sets, sewing machines, as well as all kinds of ordinary household goods, clothing and so on. They wanted to earn money because there was something to spend money on, and so they were willing to produce crops which, after they had provided enough to feed themselves, they could sell. (Robinson, 1969d, 816)

Joan Robinson made no mention of the Ten Great Relationships speech until a lecture delivered on 19 November 1969 (K.A., 1969, 5),[58] despite four visits since 1956. She did not probably know of it until she read Ch'en (1969). In her writings, she continued to think of the rightists as pro-Soviet and interpret their caution as a shortcut: "No doubt in China there are many elements in the administration and the armed forces who are attracted by the Soviet power and by modem technology; they are tempted by a short cut to industrialisation rather than going the long way by Mao's 'proletarian road'" (Robinson, 1976d, 17). She seems to have based this interpretation on Mao's post-Leap admission that "the Leap from the kingdom of necessity to the kingdom of freedom is gradually achieved in a long-term process of recognition". Her *Freedom and Necessity* (Robinson, 1970g) derived its title from this quote of Mao. It must, however, be noted here that in practice the Stalinist elements were not as visible in the rightist economic strategy as they were in the Mao line. There are, in fact, suggestions that Mao never wrote the Ten Great Relationships, which marked the break with the Soviet development strategy (Macfarquhar, 1983, 332).

During the cultural revolution, industrial breakdown did not occur because of the restructuring of the investment programme carried out by the rightists and agriculture did not produce famine conditions because of the weak incidence of the cultural revolution measures. The problem, however, was that the "communes provide complete economic security to their members, *each at the level that it has been able to attain*" [emphasis added] (Robinson, 1969b, last page). Thus the inter-commune inequality was admitted to have continued,[59] in addition to the fact that an economic base had been laid during the rightist-managed recovery after the Leap to serve as the ground for the experiment of the cultural revolution: once a society has come into being "which is providing a standard of life which may not be very comfortable but is at a level at which everybody can live; then it becomes possible to appeal to them to avoid egoism, to serve the people" (Robinson, 1970c, 46–7).

A word that does not occur anywhere in *The Cultural Revolution* is family planning. This is not surprising, as the campaign as well as the campaigners—adjudged rightist and the taking of the capitalist road—were not heard of at all during the cataclysmic years of 1966–71. This was also the period which experienced highest ever net annual increases of population (Hou Wenruo, 1981, 63). Yet Joan Robinson claimed that the security provided by the communes had weakened the old-age security hypothesis. Compared with India,[60] the propaganda for late marriage and small families was more successful because the party members "know how the people think and feel", while the campaigners in India "do not seem to be much less foreign than I would be if I went into an Indian village" (Robinson, 1969d, 818). Soon she discovered that the old-age security did not matter, at least in the countryside. Even after joining communes, peasants "positively like having babies and, when they are enjoying prosperity hitherto unknown, they find it hard to see why they should not have families of three or four at least" (Robinson, 1973f, 29).

On the basis of her writings, Joan Robinson does not emerge as a serious critic of the economic programme of the rightists. In point of fact, the success of their programme after the Leap enabled Mao to raise the questions of social equality and work ethic and motivation, which in turn lured Joan Robinson into hoping that a cooperative solution might be possible. As she put it:

> There are many elements in the conflict which arose in the Cultural Revolution. It is a very complicated affair. Clearly one element in it was the aim to give real equality of opportunity and to establish the idea that someone who contributes to the national economy as an intellectual is no more to be respected than one who contributes to the national economy by pulling a cart. (Robinson, 1970c, 44)

Such a society "is not at all an easy thing to establish". Both the capitalist and the socialist West felt the emergence of a hierarchic system "to be inescapable and therefore it is hopeless to try to contend against". The Chinese were attempting "this great experiment". Their success may not be "a hundred per cent according to the ideal. But the level which is reached, the level at which some kind of relapse sets in, is a very important matter" (Robinson, 1970c, 44–5). Her own hopes were best expressed as follows:

> The appeal to work and the organisation of employment is important not only because it overcomes hunger and misery and promises modest comfort to all before luxury to any, but also because it establishes self-respect. It is more satisfying as well as more efficient to appeal to the individual to work to 'serve the people' than to offer him 'incentive payments'. (Robinson, 1969e, 2)

These hopes soon turned into a confident assertion and even a prescription for development:

> The Cultural Revolution has been a reassertion of Mao's principles after a trend had set in towards imitating and relying upon the Soviet model. The watch-word now is 'class war, production and scientific experiment'. The revolution must be carried through by the mass of the people not by an elite, production requires hard work which will be rewarded by rising standards, scientific experiment in every sphere of life is to prevent the relapse into dogmatism and obscurantism.
>
> This is the prescription for development. No one seems to have found another way. (Robinson, 1970d, 1274)

Managing the Economic Chaos—on Rightist Principles

Economic Management (Robinson, 1973f), the result of her sixth visit, was an attempt to see how the economy of China settled down to give effect to the prescription of development emerging from the right-left struggle during the cultural revolution. Joan Robinson had arrived at a time when the campaign against "the ultra-left" and the Lin Piao incident had already taken place, enabling the pragmatic Chou En-lai and the rightists to restart normal economic activity. So the "economic management" she witnessed during her visit was again a rightist show. In the story she was told, however, there was still

> no distinction drawn between the Liu line and the ultra-left. One stood for deference, hierarchy and monetary incentives, the other for 'Down with everything', yet they are regarded as essentially the same because the consequences of both were equally counterrevolutionary. (Robinson, 1973f, 34)

In terms of economic organisation, while the Leap had essentially been about the rural sector and the communes, the cultural revolution had focused on industrial organisation. As already noted, the structure of the communes did not undergo any significant change from that enforced by the rightists in their reform of the Leap policies. The crucial distributive principle of "to each according to one's work" and the material incentive entailed by it had stayed. And so had the team as the accounting unit. Joan Robinson's confirmation was expressed as follows:

> In agriculture, for the individual, or rather the family, economic incentives are still strong, but they operate at a collective level as well as individually; the individual's share in the income of his group depends on the number of workpoints to his credit, while the value of the workpoint, in kind and in cash, depends on the production of the group. The main structure of the group has not been changed [The team] is generally the basic accounting unit. (Robinson, 1973f, 6–7)

What had somewhat changed were the systems of workpoints, varying from the very political Dazhai to the old point-price system and many mixes in between with the element of job evaluation not disregarded. Her recommendation for a producer cooperative to maximise income per man-year rather than income per unit of work[61] held in the case of communes, with the result that a perverse labour-supply response was prevented: "The fact that income received for a workpoint depends on the produce that a team gets from its own particular area of land prevents a negative response of work forthcoming to rising income. Most people, if they are free to choose, prefer to do less work as earnings per unit of effort rise." As for the question of *cui bono*, she was content to observe that "slacking by any individual is doing wrong to his neighbours by checking the rise in the value of the workpoints that all will get". While this was "another way in which Chinese institutions have been devised to promote political motivation" or collective good, the peasants "are clearly and obviously doing good for themselves at the same time" (Robinson, 1973f, 7–8).[62] There was no mention of Dazhai distributing grain by need, nor was it held out as a model to achieve inter-commune equality. There still existed rich communes and poor (*ibid.*, 13). Dazhai had taken the lead in abolishing the private plots; now she heard a rumour that even they were "thinking of re-introducing them so that the householders can have more room to keep chickens". Dazhai itself was on retreat; there was no generalisation of its policies, as she had hoped in *The Cultural Revolution*. The rightist line was back, with the family well in position. As she noted:

> The family also may have a small vegetable garden, a place to keep a pig or a sheep and some chickens, and a private plot to grow grain. The Liu Shao-chi line was to boost the household economy at the expense of the collective and in the fight against his policy there were some who advocated giving up private plots altogether, in emulation of Tachai, but the general view now is that they are useful and should be kept though not enlarged. (Robinson, 1973f, 8)

The very first attack on the Liu line was mounted against the local markets. *Economic Management* noted their re-emergence as well: "The local markets, which were heavily attacked during the struggle against the Liu line, have come back into vogue in many places." Only their scope was stated to be limited.[63] It is interesting to note that even in their heyday during the Leap, the local fairs never amounted to more than 2 per cent of the retail sales (Liu Suinian and Wu Qungan, 1986, 295). With regard to the agricultural surplus for the nonagricultural sector, Joan Robinson noted that the "private markets are now quite a minor source of supply. Before the Great Leap they were said to provide 12 per cent of total retail sales; now the estimate is 2 1/2 per cent." If anything, their role had thus increased by half a per cent after the cultural revolution over the post-Leap recovery period. Further, even after the cultural revolution, the main source of agricultural surplus—quota sales—continued to involve a set of material incentives.

In the first place, "[s]ales are made at fixed prices, which have been raised from time to time but never lowered." Second, a significant supply of agricultural surplus is "indeed, from those who nowadays are eager to sell in order to have money to buy from industry. Teams who offer to sell more than their quota of grain receive a 30 per cent premium on the price." Third, although vegetables, fruits and meat are supplied to the commerce department through contracts and not quotas, "[t]here is no problem of ensuring these supplies for the communes are eager to get contracts which provide an opportunity to earn money income all the year round". Finally, since the rightist reform of "1962, terms of trade have shifted in favour of agriculture, as the prices of the main crops have been slightly raised and the prices of many manufactures appreciably cut" (Robinson, 1973f, 12–14). In 1962, the rightists were concerned to make agriculture really the foundation to stop the repetition of the worst famine in the preceding year. In 1972, they had to deal with the overcaution of the slogan of "grain the main link", which slowed down agricultural diversification and also starved industry of its raw materials.

As pointed out earlier, the questions raised during the cultural revolution were more relevant to industry than to agriculture. These included the problem of hierarchy and elitism on the management side and of work incentive and motivation on the side of the labour. The party had always provided the leadership in the communes, but the substitution of one-man management in industry by the revolutionary committees was an important change. It gave management a representative character; its collective nature was assumed not to require any material incentives and none were given. Not only that there were no personal bonuses for managers, there were no rewards for doing better nor economic penalties for failure. Joan Robinson observed:

> Total profit is handed over to the state ... without distinction between planned and over-planned profit. A failure to achieve planned profit, unless

> for some acceptable reason, obviously would cause the management to be criticised, but it does not directly affect anyone's personal income. (Robinson, 1973f, 2–3)

Profit here refers to an element in price, the latter being given to the enterprises, together with their materials and labour. Thus to avoid "taking the capitalist road" the Chinese avoided "putting profits in command". According to Joan Robinson, "In so far as the profit criterion was used, under the influence of Liu Shao-chi, it led to anomalies." The anomaly mentioned was the determination of the product-mix by the relative rates of profit on items rather than by the composition of demand.[64] It must be remembered here that even under the Liu line implemented before the cultural revolution, prices and inputs and production plans were exogenously given to the enterprises. According to her, the difference now was that the profit as a motive was eliminated. The question is: how a production plan was implemented? In Joan Robinson's words, "carrying it out depends on self-respect and public spirit or, as the Chinese put it, on the high level of political consciousness of the workers" (*ibid.*, 4). But she also noted:

> One-man management on the Soviet model has disappeared, but the leadership of the chairman of the revolutionary committee—that is the director of an enterprise—is indispensable. As one director said with a wry smile: 'The achievements of our enterprise are due to collective work, but if anything goes wrong, it is my responsibility'. (Robinson, 1973f, 35)

Apparently, the rightists working through the National Conference on Planning (NCP) had quietly succeeded in putting in place the institution of personal responsibility in production posts. They had also slipped in a set of rules about discipline in an enterprise and a system of accounting (Liu Suinian and Wu Qungan, 1986, 379), as against the distaste voiced during the cultural revolution for accounting and "kuang-kuang", an expression for complex rules. No wonder Robinson concluded that "in tearing up the 'kuang-kuang', the workers tore up too much". The realisation had dawned on them that "because management must be simplified, it does not mean that there is no need for management [and] because irrational rules are abolished, it does not mean that there is no need for any rules" (Robinson, 1973f, 35).

There were no bonuses or payments by results for workers either. However, the euphoria during the cultural revolution "of virtually abolishing differentials altogether" had by now "been dismissed as ultra-left". Instead, an all-China three-level wage-grade system had been devised, built into which was, admitted Joan Robinson, "a certain negative monetary incentive in the desire not to miss promotion to a higher grade" (*ibid.*, 1–2).[65] She also admitted the force of the material incentive to townwards migration: "Indeed, in spite of all efforts at regulation, it is not possible altogether to eliminate infiltration into towns. Shanghai, in particular, is an irresistible attraction" (*ibid.*, 28).

Broadly the role of industrial enterprise in the Chinese system remained what Joan Robinson had always thought it to be, her fascination for the cultural revolution notwithstanding. As opposed to the East European reform, which aimed at enterprise autonomy and profitability to overcome the rigidity and inefficiency of overcentralisation, the Chinese enterprises were essentially the agents for implementing production plans prepared for them and on the basis of prices of inputs and outputs given to them. She had always held that the autonomy to determine own prices, "quite apart from the erosion of socialist morality that monetary incentives bring about", would exchange the bureaucracy of the planned system for the ailments of the market system—"monopolistic prices, advertisement, catering to tastes of higher income families and neglecting the needs of the poorer ones". The Yugoslav system was worse: profit-oriented workers could not have "an interest in providing employment for others or in evening up the level of development between regions" (*ibid.*, 3).

How the alienation of enterprises from their prices in China would, in addition to preserving socialist morality, sort out the problems of employment and inequality between persons as well as regions was not made very clear. It was clearly claimed, though, in *Economic Management* and before, that the bureaucrats in charge of commerce or internal trade were very good at ensuring a fit between supply and demand by acting as wholesalers through contracts with enterprises on the one hand and in the true interest of the consumers in their function as retailers on the other. Economic stability and consumer sovereignty were thus seen to exist by these bureaucrats. A change reported since the cultural revolution was that in some provinces, the "department" went by the planned output and consumption. It appears that the significance of this change was not fully grasped. Further decentralisation in China, as Robinson noted, had not taken place towards the enterprises but towards the provinces and localities, shedding the load of centralised ministries, including the commerce ministry, bringing to an end the so-called dictatorship of the line. That is why she was now referring to a "department" rather than a "ministry" of commerce (*ibid.*, 4–5, 22). A general effect of this decentralisation was too much capital accumulation due to a lack of proper coordination. In such a decision environment, it is difficult to see how numerous departments of commerce dealing with thousands of enterprises achieved a demand-supply fit.[66] The system is made to depend "upon a high level of morality", but while the morality of the enterprises is questioned if they have a "pecuniary interest in production"[67] through own price fixation and incentives based on sales, the morality of commerce department functionaries is impeccable as they know the "secret of carrying out development without inflation". All the same, there "is a continual campaign to prevent bureaucrats from behaving bureaucratically" (*ibid.*, 6, 20, 30).[68]

These bureaucrats were also supposed to have solved the problem existing in the Soviet sphere and stated thus: "So long as initiative and economic power lie with the producer, the enterprises are accustomed to produce what suits them and throw it on the market whether the public want it or not." However, it was also stated in the case of China: "Since the public can only choose between what already exists, it is up to the enterprise to carry out research." The suggestion here that China was not entirely free of producer initiative could scarcely be hidden in the statement of the general principle of the system "that the workers and the management of an enterprise are concerned with efficiency and quality of production, but have nothing to do with sales" (*ibid.*, 4–6). Indeed the enterprises had a hand in price fixation as well: "There are price lists for all standard products. For a new item, the producer proposes a price, based on costs, and negotiates with the buyer" (*ibid.*, 23).

However, during the economic management of the rightists, Joan Robinson was able to conclude with some satisfaction:

> There is a strong propaganda campaign for late marriage and small families. Every kind of birth control facility is available either free or at low prices in town and country. The official aim is to get the rate of population down to 1 per cent per annum. (Robinson, 1973f, 28–9)[69]

It was under the influence of the rightists that the state council formally established a family planning office in 1964. The Maoists abolished it during the cultural revolution. It was re-established only in 1973 when the rightists regained some influence (Liu Suinian and Wu Qungan, 1986, 383).

Economic Management could be summed up as an attempt by Joan Robinson to demonstrate to the world that the Chinese had carried out a great social experiment in the form of the cultural revolution, successfully absorbed its lessons regarding non-elitist management and moral incentives without affecting productivity, and were now back into the business of running a modern state with no populist hang-ups.[70] In a postscript to the second edition she outlined the "programme of economic development in China" as the raising of "productivity for the whole working population by improving health and education, by raising the fertility of the soil, by innovations in technology (whether borrowed from the West[71] or evolved at home) and by amassing an appropriate stock of equipment". As only a modest rise in living standards could be permitted to maintain the accumulation/consumption ratio, cooperative rather than competitive or planning arrangements were considered necessary to elicit the involvement of the people. She stated:

> This is an imaginative conception that has never hitherto been realised; small idealistic groups that contract out of modern commercial society usually contract out of modem productivity as well and aim at 'simple life'. In China the aim is to preserve the morality of primitive communism while introducing all the complexity of highly scientific technology in an integrated national state. (Robinson, 1975c, 42)

Joan Robinson was now beginning to recognise the existence of conflict in China more explicitly. The hitherto untried nature of the development programme in China was seen to make it inevitable. According to her, "as the programme develops, there is a right and left position on policy for the next step", the former emphasising production and the latter politics. The right was accused of resorting to shortcuts, while the left believed that "a better economic foundation will be laid and that democratic, egalitarian methods will bring more production in the end than hierarchic, bureaucratic or purely technological methods of control" (Robinson, 1975c, 42). As if to distance herself from both, she remarked: "The enormous achievements of the past twenty-five years have been the unfolding of policies conceived before Liberation, swinging a bit to the right and to the left from time to time, but never far from a central line of development" (Robinson, 1974d).

This had to be said because yet again she had been supporting a rightist economic package, this time in the first edition of *Economic Management*, only to discover later that the campaign against the ultra-left was a cover for "a swing to the right … The new campaign to criticise Confucian ideas (which are associated with the teaching of Lin Piao) is a swing the other way." This "swing back to the left" in 1974 was "reinforced in 1975 by the movement to study the dictatorship of the proletariat". A member of the Gang of Four, Wang Hongwen was quoted and the famous big character poster at Shanghai harbour—"be masters of the wharf, and not the slaves of tonnage"—was reported.

Robinson noted that many "of the criticisms heard during the Cultural Revolution are being repeated in connection" with industrial management, factory discipline and material incentives. Dismissing reports of "worse scandals" she stated: "In places where there were sharp conflicts in the last stages of the Cultural Revolution, it is expected that problems should still remain to be sorted out" (Robinson, 1975c, 43–6). It was "untrue that Mao is Utopian in the sense of promising a paradise on earth. The doctrine that 'one divides into two' means that contradictions will never end." But to suggest that Mao's thought "is something crack-brained, destined to destroy itself in the chaos that it will create", would "overlook the solid achievements that it has to its credit" (Robinson, 1975e, 273).[72]

In May 1975, she paid her last visit to China before Mao's death. Nothing that she wrote based on this experience related to the two-line struggle going on there. The objective was to see how Mao's thought affected the development of minorities. She described the treatment of national minorities as "a remarkable story of colonialism in reverse". Class war, production and scientific experiment were not imposed but shared with them. "If this is imperialism, it is very much unlike any imperialism that the world has seen before" (Robinson, 1975f, 43, h).

Like most of the previous visits, this seventh visit also coincided with a swing towards the right. In October 1974, the party central committee announced a policy of unity and stability rather than class struggle. In January 1975, Deng Xiao-ping was made vice chairman of the committee; effectively he looked after the work of the ailing Chou En-lai. A national economic plan for 1975 was put together, with the economy showing signs of recovery from the disruption of the movement to criticise Confucius and Lin Piao. Joan Robinson did not realise that "Confucius" here referred to the pragmatist Chou and was not exactly an "attack on the Confucian notion that some are born to rule and others to labour" (Robinson, 1975c, 43).

Following Mao's condemnation of the graded wage system and the principle of rewards according to work as "bourgeois rights" in February 1975, the Gang of Four built on it a campaign again by April, hastily included in the postscript to the second edition of *Economic Management* and described as "the movement to study the dictatorship of the proletariat".[73] These campaigns were stated to be meant to educate the Chinese to avoid becoming "as selfish and corrupt as" Westerners when they "become rich like them" (Robinson, 1975c, 46). However, Robinson's visit to China in May 1975 brought no first-hand information about these campaigns; she was in the deep southwest in the minority regions. Oddly enough, she did not seize on this opportunity to obtain concrete evidence for her hypothesis of inequality arising from differential rents. But she did bring back some good economic news made possible by Deng's resistance to these campaigns.

To sum up the second phase: Joan Robinson's writings on China after the Sino-Soviet ideological dispute and before the death of Mao betray a general bias towards the Maoist view of the world as well as the Maoist line on long-term development and short-term economic management in China. To some extent the bias may be understood as a sympathetic observer's attempt to counterbalance the often ill-informed and one-sided view of China in a world dominated by the US policy to isolate China, and joined subsequently by a hostile Soviet Union; whether her counterbalancing exercise was based on superior access to information is another matter. Her denial of the famine in 1961, dismissiveness of any significant retreat from the Great Leap, a complete innocence of the power struggle during the cultural revolution and the Lin Piao affair suggest she perhaps knew no better than those assumed by her to be ill-informed. In fact no information was published by China since the disasters of the Leap. Curiously, she justified this blackout.[74] On top of it she stated that it was not difficult to get information about China: "In fact, anyone who wants to can find out a great deal. The difficulty is not in knowing what is going on, but in believing it" (Robinson, 1970d, 1267).

Small wonder, her reports often contained a certain anticipation of being doubted.[75] Nevertheless, as this chapter has shown, underlying the commitment to support Maoist China on a political level was a set of economic policies which she thought were consistent with her own ideas and which kept the economy going through thick and thin. Ironically, the Chinese propaganda machine dubbed these policies as rightist. The only time Joan Robinson became a leftist in the Chinese context was during the cultural revolution. Like many in the world she for once believed that a cooperative, selfless and unbureaucratic socioeconomic organisation was possible. It was the failure of the cultural revolution as a grand social experiment, and the thought of being disinformed about its real motives and actual developments, that led to the phase of self-criticism discussed in the next chapter.

Notes

1. See Brammall's doctoral dissertation at the University of Cambridge (1989).
2. What Joan Robinson called Marxist orthodoxy was not exclusive to China. The Soviet Union and North Korea did not encourage family

planning. Cuba encouraged it "only mildly" (Robinson, 1965d, 545, 1966b, 17).

3. Robinson (1964c, 9) mentions seven different districts and Robinson (1964d, 5) states the number of provinces to be four.
4. Joan Robinson was not oblivious of the fact that a number of brigades and some communes were also the basic accounting unit (Robinson, 1964e, 289). It was not "a Bed of Procrustes into which everyone is thrust" (Robinson, 1964b, 201).
5. I am grateful to Liu Minquan for allowing me to see parts of the research-in-progress for his doctoral dissertation for the University of Oxford.
6. The same author, reviewing Robinson (1964h) in the same place, noted that though "she deliberately seeks to present the Chinese viewpoint as a corrective to the flood of hostile comment she overdoes the whitewashing" (Hayward, 1966, 98–9).
7. She was confused about the procurement prices of fruits and vegetables, sometimes "settled in advance, but selling prices to the public vary" and at others "procurement prices are lowered" (Robinson, 1964c, 8, d, 6).
8. As vegetable production is more profitable than grain, she also noted that the Chinese economists were debating the issue of socialist rent and the techniques of mopping it up without disturbing the incentives. "For the time being it lies where it falls" (Robinson, 1964d, 6). As Zhong (1961) noted: "[T]he differential rent attributable to land with favourable natural conditions should, in general, be kept by production teams concerned." See Nolan (1983c) for a discussion of differential rent and distributional change.
9. See also Robinson (1971b).
10. Liu Suinian and Wu Qungan (1986, 241–2).
11. The special issue of the Bulletin of the Atomic Scientists on China, which reproduced Robinson (1964d) as Robinson (1966c), also carried an article by Gray (1966), which did suggest, albeit in a sympathetic tone, that the movement towards collectivisation was not consistent with the declared aim of gradualism.
12. See Yuming Sheng's doctoral dissertation, University of Cambridge.
13. Quoting Che Guevara she observed "that in Latin America the Chinese point of view corresponds more closely to experience than the Russian" (Robinson, 1964f, 238).
14. Indeed, she was so enamoured by the new Chinese strategy that she started to prescribe it to other developing countries. For instance, she

told Pakistanis that the Chinese principle of walking on both legs was "very clearly" applicable to their economy (Robinson, 1964i, 6).

15. Even before China, according to Joan Robinson, the North Koreans departed from the Soviet model. The first three years of their seven-year plan stressed basic needs, allowing "the authorities [to] go all out for expansion of basic industries again" in the remaining period of the plan (Robinson, 1965d, 543). However, Joan Robinson saw it as a continuing strategy in China, rather than the North Korean's tactical retreat. This "sharp break" was noted in the case of Cuba as well (Robinson, 1966b, 13). Preece (1968, 297), however, considered the Chinese experience as confirming the correctness of heavy industry priority.
16. "I was inclined to doubt whether this could really be true until I saw something of what technical self-reliance has done for North Korea" (Robinson, 1965c, 11).
17. She also held the Chinese brief in the Sino-Indian border conflict. A great admirer of the Indian intellectuals' "capacity for detachment", she had to "admit that it wore a bit thin in autumn of 1962" (Robinson, 1967a, 111).
18. See Robinson (1942b, 1951b). See also Robinson (1952b) and a denunciation of it in *Times Literary Supplement* on 25 July 1952, titled "Mrs. Robinson's Sprightly Conference Sketch Book" (485).
19. See *New York Times,* 27 June 1952. See also Robinson (1953b, c, 1956f, 1960f).
20. 13 June 1953.
21. *The Economist,* 28 November 1953.
22. The reference to "a Chinese friend" in Robinson (1952b, 6) and to "C" in Robinson (1954a, 24) is to Chi Chao-ting.
23. She would vote Labour but was not a "Labourite economist". See Turner (1989, 210, 241). A Labour Party card forms part of the JVR Collection, King's College, Cambridge.
24. *Broadsheet* (January 1964, 1).
25. *Broadsheet* (March 1964, 1).
26. The Soviet position was not stated fairly. See Churchward (1966, 100). Even a decade later, the Soviet propaganda seemed to her to partly "reflect Russian envy that in China the peasantry is being absorbed into socialism and the production of food keeps ahead of the growth of population" (Robinson, 1976d, 17).
27. The bomb was supported against her general stance of pacifism (Robinson, 1965c, 14–15).

28. Needham (1965, 2, 1985, 19–20). Author's interview with Ronald Berger, 20 February (1987).
29. A Marxist and author of *From Marx to Mao Tse-tung*, published by the China Policy Study Group (CPSG) in 1971.
30. *Broadsheet* (December 1981, 1).
31. See Gittings (1985, 23). See also *China Now*, May–June 1980, which deals with "advance or retreat" after Mao.
32. This is a recurrent theme of her *Economic Philosophy* (Robinson, 1962a).
33. The reference here is to Yang Hsien-chen's idea of dialectics as a quest for unity and reconciliation and Mao's theory of continuing conflict and contradiction under socialism.
34. Robinson (1965c, 11).
35. Although no bigger than the erstwhile lower-form cooperative, the team still comprised 30–40 households (Robinson, 1968e, 685), a size considered not so small by Peter Nolan.
36. See Liu Suinian and Wu Qungan (1986, 241–334).
37. Page references to Robinson (1973a), which reproduces Robinson (1967h).
38. Ajit Singh's letter to the author, 6 January (1989). See also Singh (1979, 592–3). Paine (1974, 91) too believed that Joan Robinson's description of the system showed how China avoided Soviet-type queuing.
39. See Robinson (1964l, 80–1, m, 493, g, 2, h, 89–91, g, 46–50, h, 40–7). See also Robinson (1970g, 102–4, f, 3–5) and Robinson and Eatwell (1973, 320–1).
40. Joan Robinson's interest in the cultural revolution presents an interesting contrast with the "cultural evolution" perspective of her *Economic Philosophy* and an interest in the work of Ayres. See Aires (1944) and JVR Collection, viii/Ayres. King's College, Cambridge. See also Phillips (1971, 354–8).
41. Later he described the cultural revolution as "a veritable heresy of Maoist ideology" and "a great and horrible mistake" (Needham, 1978, 832, 1985, 20).
42. *SACU News,* December 1967.
43. JVR Collection, ii/36. King's College, Cambridge. In Robinson (1978e, 62) she observed: "Along with the concept of freedom goes freedom of the market, and the philosophy of orthodox economics is that the pursuit of self-interest will lead to the benefit of society. By this means the moral problem is abolished. The moral problem is concerned with the conflict between individual interest and the interest of society."

44. A number of development economists, who became concerned about income distribution and rural development at the start of the seventies, "looked to China as a possible model" (Perkins, 1983, 345).
45. For whose benefit?
46. Tintner and Peek (1976, 374–5), after pinpointing the lack of a systematic view of cooperation based on New Left values, refer to Joan Robinson's *Economic Management* to state that "Usually the point is made that such a system presently prevails in China." *Economic Management,* however, does not contain a clearly expressed theory of cooperation. It merely describes the Chinese system after the cultural revolution. Joan Robinson did not develop any systematic theory of capitalist inequality. For her views on distribution under different systems, see Robinson (1967k).
47. Robinson (1972a) was more explicit—"For use, not for profit" was its title.
48. No. 49 (1967, 15).
49. Mao's interview with Snow was published in *The Sunday Times,* 2 May 1971.
50. Later she admitted that "we all had a lot of wind in our heads" during the cultural revolution (Robinson, 1978c, 4).
51. The capitalists receiving interest on the value of their former assets and those given executive positions "melted in the fire of the Cultural Revolution" (Robinson, 1969a, 125).
52. Although the purge denied before had taken place and the "chief heretic" (Robinson, 1965c, 12) was no more in the job, she satisfied herself by saying that it was not a Stalin-style purge (Robinson, 1969a, 20). According to Macfarquhar, "a generation of leaders disappeared. They did not go to their deaths as had Stalin's victims; but they were denounced not merely for mistakes during the years prior to cultural revolution, but for actions spanning their entire careers. Their contributions to the Chinese revolution were denied; their lifetimes of dedicated work were declared null and void" (1974, 3).
53. For suggesting that "[t]he thought of Mao Tse-tung may curdle into strange forms when it is injected into other civilisations" (Robinson, 1968b, 5), the British equivalent of the Red Guards called her "a hireling of the capitalist class" (*SACU News,* June–July 1968, 4). She retorted by describing them as "ultra-left" (Robinson, 1968d, 5), a label that would later be used for the Chinese Red Guards as well.

54. The reference is to the following statement issued by Hisinhua on 15 March 1968: "China's Khrushchev said, with ulterior motives: 'Do as the masses want' and 'mainly depend on the spontaneity of the mass movement'. Such statements as these plainly show how he opposed the Party leadership and peddled anarchism."
55. One reviewer remarked: "There is a certain sadness in seeing so eminent a scholar reduced to saying that a statement was 'not intended as a contribution to historical analysis' when what is meant is that it was a blatant lie" (Bell, 1969, 339).
56. For instance, she remarked in the case of Sri Lanka that the trouble with its "economy has not been too much exploitation but too little" (Robinson, 1959, 71).
57. Riskin (1987, 184–6) talks of useless industrial production, sluggish agriculture and "unknown degrees of statistical exaggeration".
58. This lecture was published as Robinson (1970d) and reproduced as Robinson (1970e, 1971a).
59. On the seriousness of this problem, see Nolan (1983c).
60. Comparisons were often drawn with India. For instance, while agreeing with Beckerman on the desirability of growth, she asked: "Has he compared the slums of Calcutta with the neat housing estates of Shanghai?" (Robinson, 1974f, 20).
61. Robinson (1967b, 222–3).
62. As noted above, the work of Liu Minquan (1989, 1990) shows that views like that of Joan Robinson on labour supply and incentives are seriously flawed.
63. "It is forbidden to deal in produce that comes under the state plan—grain, oil seeds, cotton etc.—it is forbidden to buy for re-sale and there is a ceiling to every price. Under the ceiling, prices are settled by supply and demand. Households can sell their private produce and handicrafts and the team may sell fruit and vegetables outside their regular contracts" (Robinson, 1973f, 9).
64. She also underscored the impossibility of working "out such a delicate system of profit ratios as to get exactly the desirable product mix" (Robinson, 1973f, 3).
65. *The Times* of 26 June 1972 headlined a wage hike with effect from July 1971 thus: "China returns material incentives to worker." Joan Robinson footnoted the heading, where she mentioned the wage hike in Robinson (1972a, 6). While the last-mentioned article formed part of *Economic*

Management, the paragraph which mentions the wage hike is without the footnote about the material incentives (Robinson, 1973f, 2). In Robinson (1972b, 132), the news about the restoration of material incentives in industry is dismissed as a rumour.

66. Capital accumulation jumped up from 23.2 per cent in 1969 to 32.9 and 34.1 per cent in 1970 and 1971 respectively. Again in 1971, wage payments and foodgrain sales—demand—dangerously exceeded consumer goods and marketable grain—supply. See Liu Suinian and Wu Qungan (1986, 374–5).
67. Rawsski (1975, 758) finds this "assertion" to be "a dubious suggestion which is contradicted by subsequent passages linking profits with investment".
68. It was recognised that "bureaucracy [in China] is performing the functions, not only of the civil service in the capitalist countries, but also a large part of private business" (Robinson, 1973f, 20).
69. See also Robinson (1974c, 3).
70. In August 1974 she announced: "My traveller's tales from Asia … were at first greeted with scepticism, but recently many observers have confirmed them and I am now quite in fashion" (Robinson, 1975b, xiv).
71. "In 1973, the rightist influence led to the import of 13 giant chemical fertiliser plants, four giant chemical fibre mills, 3 petroleum chemical industrial works, one alkyl benzene works, 43 sets of coal combines, three giant power stations and the 1.7 metre rolling machine for Wuhan Steel" (Liu Suinian and Wu Qungan (1986, 384).
72. Introducing a pamphlet on education, she noted the ascendancy of the Liu line—"a policy of developing a privileged elite"—during the post-Leap recovery and the struggle in the cultural revolution to return to Mao's ideals: "The most important part of education in China is outside the schools. The Thought of Mao Tse-tung is not only moral and political but also an appeal to apply the scientific method in daily life" (1975d, 1).
73. Hastily because it is only mentioned once at the end, occurs in a section titled "Postscript—summer 1974" despite being a 1975 development, with "1975" slipped in at the last stages of printing indicated by unusual spacing (Robinson, 1975c, 46), and the fact that she was about to leave for China on her seventh trip.
74. "Clearly they have statistics, though they don't publish any central overall statistics. Why don't they? Well, why should they? I don't think they lose anything by not publishing" (Robinson, 1968e, 691–2).

75. For instance, "Why should you believe me when I tell you this? The press often gives you quite a different story." Another instance: "Hostile observers (including many professional China-watchers) like to discredit the reports of visitors who, they maintain, must have been shown around" (Robinson, 1969d, 817, 1970f, 9).

References

Unpublished Material

Ajit Singh's letter to the author, 6 January, 1989.

Brammall, C.M. (1989) Inequality and Poverty in Rural China: The Case of Sichuan Province, 1931–1978. Unpublished PhD dissertation, University of Cambridge.

Interview with Ronald Berger, 20 February, 1987.

Published Works

Adler, S. (1957) *The Chinese Economy*. London: Routledge and Kegan Paul.

Aird, John S. (1972) 'Population Policy and Demographic Prospects in the People's Republic of China,' in *People's Republic of China: An Economic Assessment. Joint Economic Committee, Congress of the United States (1972)*, 220–331. Washington, DC: U.S. Government Printing Office.

———. (1982) 'Population Studies and Population Policy in China,' *Population and Development Review*, 8(2), 267–97.

Aires, C.E. (1944) *The Theory of Economic Progress*. Chapel Hill: University of North Carolina Press.

Ashton, B., et al. (1984) 'Famine in China, 1958–61,' *Population and Development Review*, 10, 613–45.

Bell, C. (1969) 'The Debate on China,' *Political Quarterly*, 40, 337–43.

Caute, D. (1977) *The Fellow-travellers*. London: Quartet Books.

Chen, Chi-yi. (1964) *La Reforme Agraire en Chine Populaire*. The Hague: Mouton.

Ch'en, J. (1969) *Mao*. Englewood Cliffs, NJ: Prentice Hall.

Churchward, L.G. (1966) 'Review of Robinson (1964h),' *Science and Society*, 30, 100–2.

Coale, A. (1984) *Rapid Population Change in China 1952–1982*. Washington, DC: National Academy of Sciences Press.
Crook, I. and D. Crook. (1965) *The First Years of Yang-yi Commune*. London: Routledge and Kegan Paul.
Domar, E. (1966) 'The Soviet Collective Farm as a Producer Cooperative,' *American Economic Review*, 56, 734–57.
Dumonr, R. (1966) *La Chine Surpleuplee, Tiers Monde Affame*. Editions du Seuil.
Gittings, J. (1985) 'From Brickbats to Bonhomie,' *China Now*, 114, 21–3.
Gray, J. (1966) 'China Today: Agrarian Policies,' *Bulletin of the Atomic Scientists*, 22, 32–9.
Hayward, J.E.S. (1966) 'Leninizing China and Sinicizing Lenin,' *Political Studies*, 14, 95–9.
Hou Wenruo. (1981) 'Population Policy,' in Liu Zheng, et al. (eds.), *China's Population: Problems and Prospects*. Beijing: New World Press, 55–76.
K.A. (1969) 'An Economist Sums Up,' *SACU News*, 6, 5.
Karol, K.S. (1975) *The Second Chinese Revolution*. London: Jonathan Cape.
Liu Minquan. (1989) *Work Incentives in the Production Team in Southern Jiangsu, China, 1960s–70s*. Ld'A-QEH Development Studies Working Paper No. 10, University of Oxford.
———. (1990) *Incentives and Labour Under the Communes in China*. In progress PhD dissertation, University of Oxford.
Liu Suinian and Wu Qungan. (eds.) (1986) *China's Socialist Economy: An Outline History*. Beijing: Beijing Review Press.
Macfarquhar, R. (1974) *The Origins of The Cultural Revolution. 1: Contradictions among the People 1956–1957*. London: Oxford University Press.
———. (1983) *The Origins of The Cultural Revolution. Vol. 2. The Great Leap Forward 1958–1960*. London: Oxford University Press.
Needham, J. (1965) 'SACU: A Genuine Effort Towards Understanding,' *SACU News*, 1, 1–2.
———. (1978) 'Rise and Fall of the Anti-Intellectual "Gang",' *Nature*, 274, 832–4.
———. (1985) 'The President Looks Back,' *China Now*, 114, 19–20.
Nolan, P. (1983c) *Growth Processes and Distributional Change in a South Chinese Province: The Case of Guangdong*. London: Contemporary China Institute.
———. (1988) *The Political Economy of Collective Farms: An Analysis of China's Post-Mao Reform*. Cambridge: Polity Press.
Paine, S. (1974) 'Review of *The Chinese Road to Socialism*,' in E.L. Wheelwright and B. McFarlane (eds.), *Conference of Socialist Economists*, Spring, 3, 91–2.

Perkins, D.H. (1983) 'Research on the Economy of the People's Republic of China: A Survey of the Field,' *Journal of Asian Studies*, 42, 345–78.
Perkins, D.H. and S. Yusuf. (1984) *Rural Development in China*. Baltimore: The Johns Hopkins University Press for World Bank.
Phillips, C.S. Jr. (1971) 'The Revival of Cultural Evolution in Social Science Theory,' *Journal of Developing Areas*, 5, 337–70.
Preece, P.F.W. (1968) 'The Priority Given to Heavy Industry in Socialist Economic Planning, *Science and Society*, 32, 288–99.
Rawsski, T.G. (1975) 'Review of Robinson (1975c),' *China Quarterly*, 64, 756–8.
Riskin, C. (1987) *China's Political Economy: The Quest for Development Since 1949*. New York: Oxford University Press.
Robinson, Joan. (1942b) ' Review of L.E. Hubbard, *Soviet Labour and Industry*,' *Cambridge Review*, 63, 348–9.
———. (1951b) 'Preparation for War,' Reprinted from *Cambridge Today* in *Monthly Review*, 3, 194–5.
———. (1952b) *Conference Sketch Book*. Cambridge: Heifer.
———. (1953b) 'On Trade with Russia,' Letter to *The Times*, 1 September, 7.
———. (1953c) 'East-West Trade,' Letter to *The Times*, 15 September, 7.
———. (1953d) 'A Mission to Moscow,' Letter to *The Economist*, 28 November, 655.
———. (1953e) Letter to *The Economist*, 5 December, 742.
———. (1954a) *Letters from a Visitor to China*. Cambridge: Students' Bookshops.
———. (1956f) 'British-Soviet Trade Prospects,' *British-Soviet Friendship*, October.
———. (1959) 'Economic Possibilities of Ceylon,' in *Papers by Visiting Economists*, 38–71. Colombo: National Planning Council.
———. (1960f) 'East-West Trade,' Letter to *The Economist*, 16 January, 195.
———. (1962a) *Economic Philosophy*. London: C.A. Watts.
———. (1962b) 'Review of E.S. Kirby (ed.),' *Contemporary China. Economic Journal*, 72, 734.
———. (1964a) 'Communes in China,' *Listener*, 71, 177–89.
———. (1964b) 'Notes from China,' *Economic Weekly*, 16, 195–203.
———. (1964c) 'A British Economist on Chinese Communes,' *Eastern Horizon*, 3, 6–11.
———. (1964d) 'Chinese Agricultural Communes,' *Coexistence*, 1, 1–6.
———. (1964e) 'The Chinese Communes,' *Political Quarterly*, 35, 285–97.
———. (1964f) 'The Chinese Point of View,' *International Affairs*, 40, 232–44.

———. (1964g) 'Prospects for China,' *New Scientist*, 22, 756.
———. (1964h) *Notes from China*. Oxford: Basil Blackwell.
———. (1964i) 'Planning for Economic Development,' *Trade Journal* (Pakistan), June–July, 5–7.
———. (1964l) 'Consumer's Sovereignty in a Planned Economy,' in *On Political Economy and Econometrics: Essays in Honour of Oskar Lange*. Oxford: Pergman Press. Also in Robinson (I965a), 70–81.
———. (1964m) 'Review of H.G. Shaffer (ed.),' *The Soviet Economy. Cambridge Review*, 85, 491–2.
———. (1965c) 'What's New in China?' *Eastern Horizon*, 4, 11–5.
———. (1965d) 'Korean Miracle,' *Monthly Review*, 16 (9), 541–9.
———. (1965g) 'Economic Principles in China,' Review of C. Bettelheim, et al., *Construction du Socialisme en Chine, Broadsheet*, 2, 1–3.
———. (1965h) Review of P.J.D. Wiles, *The Political Economy of Communism*, in Robinson, (1965a), 82–91.
———. (1966a) 'Review of Walker (1965),' *International Affairs*, 42, 159–60.
———. (1966b) 'Cuba—1965,' *Monthly Review*, 17, 10–18.
———. (1966c) 'China Today: The Organisation of Agriculture,' *Bulletin of the Atomic Scientists*, 22, 28–32.
———. (1966d) 'Organisation of Agriculture,' in R. Adams (ed.), *Contemporary China*. London: Peter Owen.
———. (1966e) 'Reviews of Chen Chi-yi, *La Reforme Agraire en Chine Populaire;* Yuan-li Wu. *The Steel Industry In Communist China*,' *International Affairs*, July 42, 546–8.
———. (1966f) 'Review of C. Bettelheim, et al., La Construction du Socialisme en Chine,' *Coexistence*, 3, 105–7.
———. (1966g) 'The Communes and the Great Leap Forward,' Reviews of Crook and Crook (1965); Dumont (1966). *New Left Review*, 37, 69–72.
———. (1966h) *Economics: An Awkward Corner*. London: George Allen and Unwin.
———. (1967a) 'Contribution to Sanity,' Letter. *Economic and Political Weekly*, 2, 111.
———. (1967b) 'The Soviet Collective Farm as a Producer Cooperative: Comment,' *American Economic Review*, 57(1), 222–3.
———. (1967g) 'The Economic Reforms,' *Monthly Review*, 19, 45–50.
———. (1967h) 'Socialist Affluence,' in C.H. Feinstein (ed.), *Socialism, Capitalism and Economic Growth: Essays in Honour of Maurice Dobb*. London: Cambridge University Press. Also in Robinson, (1973a), 33–47.
———. (1967k) 'Growth and the Theory of Distribution,' *Annals of Pubic and Co-operative Economics*, 38(1), 3–7.

———. (1968a) 'Review of Jan Myrdal,' *Report from a Chinese Village, International Affairs*, 44, 152–3.
———. (1968b) 'Intensive Look at China,' *SACU News*, 3, 1–5.
———. (1968c) 'The Cultural Revolution in China,' *International Affairs*, 44, 214–27.
———. (1968d) 'Reply to Sussex Internationalists' Attack, *SACU News*, 3, 5.
———. (1968e) 'China Today: Economic Organisation,' *Journal of the Royal Society of Arts*, 116, 683–93.
———. (1968h) 'The Decentralised Society. Review of A. Donnithorne,' *China's Economic System, SACU News*, 5.
———. (1969a) *The Cultural Revolution in China*. Harmondsworth, Middlesex: Penguin Books.
———. (1969b) 'Ten Years of Communes,' *Broadsheet*, 6, 3.
———. (1969d) 'India and China: A Comparison,' *Listener*, 82, 816–18.
———. (1969e) 'Preface,' in N. Brunner (ed.), *China's Economy*. London: Anglo-Chinese Educational Institute, 1–2.
———. (1969f) Letter to *Tribune*, 24 January.
———. (1970c) 'Society and Economics in China Today,' in R. Jungk, et al., *China and the West: Mankind Evolving*. London: Granstone Press, 35–47.
———. (1970d) 'Chinese Economic Policy,' *Studium Generale*, 23, 1267–74.
———. (1970e) 'Chinese Economic Policy: Prescription for Development,' *China Now*, 4, 5–8.
———. (1970f) 'Foreword,' in E.L. Wheelwright and B. McFarlane (eds.), *The Chinese Road to Socialism*. New York: Monthly Review Press.
———. (1970g) *Freedom and Necessity*. London: George Allen and Unwin.
———. (1971a) 'Chinese Economic Policy,' in J. Needham, et al., *Hand and Brain in China and Other Essays*. London: Anglo-Chinese Educational Institute, 19–27.
———. (1971b) 'Something to Live for. Review of J. Myrdal and G. Kessle,' *The Revolution Continued New Statesman*, 81, 631–3.
———. (1972a) 'For Use, Not for Profit,' *Eastern Horizon*, 11, 6–15.
———. (1972b) 'Through Western Spectacles,' Reviews of K. Mehnert, *China Today*; Terrill (1972); and K. Ling, *Red Guard, Spectator*, 7522, 321.
———. (1973a) *Collected Economic Papers*, Vol. 4. Oxford: Basil Blackwell.
———. (1973f) *Economic Management in China, 1972*. London: Anglo-Chinese Educational Institute.
———. (1974c) 'Achievements of a Generation,' *China Now*, 45, 2–3.
———. (1974d) 'Two Revolutions,' *Broadsheet*, 11, 4.
———. (1974f) 'On the Pollyanna of Economic Growth. Review of W. Beckerman,' *In Defence of Economic Growth, Spectator*, 7619, 19–20.

———. (1974h) "Inflation and Stabilisation: A Neo-Keynesian View,' *Spectator*, 19 October 1974h, 7634, 488–9.
———. (1975b) 'Introduction 1974: Comments and Explanations,' in *Collected Economic Papers*, Vol. 3, 2nd ed. Oxford: Basil Blackwell, iii–xiv.
———. (1975c) *Economic Management in China*. 2nd ed. London: Anglo-Chinese Educational Institute.
———. (1975d) 'Foreword,' in P. Mauger et al., *Education in China*. London: Anglo-Chinese Educational Institute, 1–2.
———. (1975e) Review of Leslie R. Marchant,' *To Phoenix Seat: An Introductory Study of Maoism and the Chinese Communist Quest for a Paradise on Earth, History*, 60, 272–3.
———. (1975f) 'National Minorities in Yunnan,' *Eastern Horizon*, 14, 32–43.
———. (1975h) 'Hsishuang Parma,' *China Now*, 55, 10–11, 15–16.
———. (1975i) 'The Fall of Lin Piao.' Review of P. Worsley, *Inside China*; K.S. Karol, *The Second Chinese Evolution, Spectator*, 7677, 217.
———. (1976d) 'Walled in,' Review of E.S. Kirby, *Russian Studies of China, Spectator*, 7699, 17.
———. (1978c) 'China 1978: Comments on Bettelheim,' *China Now*, 80, 4–7.
———. (1978e) 'Morality and Economics,' *Challenge*, 21, 62–4.
———. (1982) 'Introduction,' *China Now*, 100, 3.
Robinson, Joan and S. Adler. (1958) *China: An Economic Perspective*. London: Fabian International Bureau, Fabian Tract No. 314.
Robinson, Joan and R. Berger. (1961) 'Thinking about China: The Economic Impact of Communism,' *Listener*, 2 February 1961, 65, 220–2.
Robinson, Joan and J. Eatwell. (1973) *An Introduction to Modern Economics*. London: McGraw-Hill.
Singh, A. (1979) 'The "Basic Needs" Approach to Development vs the New International Order: The Significance of Third World Industrialisation,' *World Development*, 7, 585–606.
Skinner, G.W. (1965) 'Marketing and Social Structure in China, Part III,' *Journal of Asian Studies*, 24, 363–99.
Tintner, G. and P. Peek. (1976) 'Marginalism and Linear Economics East and West,' *History of Political Economy*, 8, 367–79.
Turner, M.S. (1989) *Joan Robinson and the Americans*. Armonk, NY: M.E. Sharpe.
Walker, K.R. (1965) *Planning in Chinese Agriculture*. Chicago: Aldine.
Ward, B. (1958) 'The Firm in Illyria: Market Syndicalism,' *American Economic Review*, 48, 566–89.
Zhong, C.Z. (1961) 'On Differential Rent in China's Rural Communes,' *Red Flag*, 1 December.

5

The Third Phase: Self-criticism

In 1976, while still critical "of old China-watchers",[1] a turning point came when Joan Robinson for the first time asked some questions about the cultural revolution:

> Was unleashing the Cultural Revolution a colossal gamble? Was the gamble too rash? Indeed, the fact that it led up to the Lin Piao affair makes one shudder. But as recent events show, the two line struggle will never end. (Robinson, 1976b, 51)[2]

Looking Back—With the Benefit of Hindsight

The time had come to look back; a selection of writings based on Robinson's seven visits during 1953–75, appropriately described as Reports from China, candidly admitted:

> I have had the good fortune to be able to visit the People's Republic of China a number of times over the last quarter of century, first in 1953. I have no special knowledge of Chinese history and none at all of the language; I am very far from being an "authority"; yet I thought it a duty to

P. Tahir, *Making Sense of Joan Robinson on China*, Palgrave Studies in the History of Economic Thought, https://doi.org/10.1007/978-3-030-28825-9_5

> tell the world whatever I could. I therefore decided to write down, very naively, just what I saw in China and what I felt at the time. Now that so many visitors are going from the West, it may be of interest to see some earlier impressions, and some reflections of the dramatic changes that China had been going through before they began to come. (Robinson, 1977a, 7)

What is made clear is that her writings recorded impressions and reflections; they were not authoritative analyses. The selection pattern is suggestive. The first and the last report based on the first and the last visit to China under Mao show, respectively, her enthusiastic first impressions of the Chinese revolution and its impact on minorities.[3] No significant comment is made on them. The second report is stated to be missing. In place of it, reminiscences of the period are provided. No attempt is made to make any significant comment here either. Note was, however, now taken of the anti-right campaign (Robinson, 1977a, 38–9). It was noted above that Robinson and Adler (1958), a publication based on the experience of her (and Adler's) visit to China in 1957, disregarded this campaign entirely. It was also argued that the main ideas emerging from it were closer to the viewpoint of the rightists. The third visit is represented by a merger of parts of Robinson (1964a, c) under the title "Economic Recovery". This is a recognition of the success of the rightist economic package launched after the disasters of the Leap, a perspective which at that time had been overshadowed by her fascination with the communes—"a brilliant invention in agricultural organisation". A postscript noted, however, that the "whole economy and the whole system has come a long way since 1963, but the main structure of the communes has not changed and they are proving to be a remarkably successful way of bringing socialism in the organisation of agriculture" (Robinson, 1977a, 7, 55).

The communes had been restructured by the rightists in 1963. This re-affirms the view presented here that the underlying economic message of the early visits of Joan Robinson did not suggest a significant variance from the development strategy devised by the rightists in China. An observation made in Robinson (1964b) and now repeated under the heading of "Economic policy" stated: "The dogmatism that appears in Chinese propaganda to the world is in no way reflected in internal policy, which is empirical and follows economic commonsense" (Robinson, 1977a, 43). The tribute to the rightist economic policies is obvious. The observation also helps explain her comment introducing Robinson (1964c)—"the Chinese point of view"—that she "understood China's foreign policy then better than … now, in 1976" (Robinson, 1977a, 7). Thus the major works during the first phase—the *Letters* and *Economic Perspective*[4]—were spared any serious self-criticism.

What she still did not fully comprehend now, nor at the time of the occurrence, was the cultural revolution. As noted before, she had begun to ask questions, though. Robinson (1965), written after her quick visit to China and North Korea,[5] had discounted the possibility of a purge suggested by other Western writers. The purge of course took place later during the cultural revolution, when Liu was removed from the scene. The report was now described as "rather superficial. At that time there were symptoms, which I did not quite take in, of the spread of Confucian attitudes that made the Cultural Revolution necessary" (Robinson, 1977a, 7–8).

So the cultural revolution was necessary, but Robinson's attempt in *The Cultural Revolution* (Robinson, 1969) "to find the meaning of the Cultural Revolution is obviously superficial too,[[6]] but it throws some light on the origin of the struggle between two lines, especially in education and industry, which has broken surface afresh". The reference here is to the death of Chou En-lai in 1976, after which the

> unresolved conflicts broke out again. Indeed, it is impossible that the 'struggle between two lines' should ever be finally settled. In administration there can never be a completely satisfactory balance between the requirements of good order and proper bureaucratic procedures on the one side and democratic spontaneity on the other, or, in education, between the claims of academic standards and of the widest possible spread of opportunity. (*Ibid.*, 8, 119)

The above was stated in a postscript added to a reproduction of parts of *The Cultural Revolution* and an amalgam of some passages of its own postscript with three pages from *Economic Management* (Robinson, 1973, 32–4). Although the postscript seems to have been written after the death of Mao and the arrest of the Gang of Four, Joan Robinson was content with a brief statement: "Now, in the spring of 1977 a new chapter is opening, but whatever happens next, the lessons that the people learned in the Cultural Revolution will still be remembered" (Robinson, 1977a, 119–20). What were these lessons? The two-line struggle in education and industry was stated to be never-ending. *Economic Management*, which she based on "a period of reconciliation and transformation after the great upheaval", during which she tried "to make a study of Chinese methods of planning and industrial organisation" (*ibid.*, 1977a, 8), did not at the end lead to any clear-cut lessons. What she had imagined to be a sober attempt to implement the lessons of the cultural revolution in industry and education was in point of fact a rightist effort to keep the economy going. In agriculture, the two-line struggle was not considered serious, as the structure of communes as a way of organising agriculture had remained more or less intact. But that was not a lesson of the cultural revolution, but a policy reform introduced by the rightists after the disasters of the Leap. Basically Joan Robinson had to repudiate *The Cultural Revolution* and what was based on its supposed lessons, *Economic Management*, as more information became available.

Joan Robinson After Mao

After the death of Mao, a lively debate took place about the future course of Chinese development, especially among those who had been sympathetic to the Maoist line. Bettelheim, who had written a well-known book on the cultural revolution[7] and was the president of the Franco-Chinese Friendship Association (FCFA), resigned from that body in May 1977, declined to visit China and wrote a lengthy piece to argue that China since Mao had taken a "great leap backward" (Beitelheim, 1978a, b). Joan Robinson did not become cynical. She continued as the vice-president of SACU and as a sponsor of the China Policy Study Group (CPSG) visited China in May 1978, held discussions with the new leadership and wrote a rebuttal to Bettelheim. She had never been shy of admitting that the external propaganda by the Chinese was dogmatic.[8] Now she also admitted that

> the content and style of Chinese internal propaganda is very misleading when read from a Western point of view. I sympathise to a certain extent with Bettelheim's initial reaction. I think we all had a lot of wind in our heads; it was hard to believe that, in a socialist country, policy could have been the sport of personal ambition and it was deflating to be told that the Cultural Revolution is over. (Robinson, 1978a, 4)

She recognised that the propaganda in the past had been "heavily monolithic—101 per cent one way or the other—and therefore unenlightening". She maintained that she had "always taken every opportunity to make these points and, in 1978, … found more ready listeners than ever before". The decade of 1966–76 had "been a profound shock. How could it happen that, under cover of Mao Tsetung Thought, a medieval drama of ambition and treachery could play itself out?"[9] The lesson of the cultural revolution was now unambiguously stated:

> The rise and fall of Lin Piao and of Chiang Ching has given [the Chinese] a sharp lesson. They are beginning to realise that their main danger is not so much the temptations of the capitalist road as their ingrained Confucian respect for hierarchy. The Cultural Revolution was a violent effort to break out of it which ran off the rails. (Robinson, 1978a, 7)

The above quote lends support to the conclusion here that Joan Robinson did not have any serious problems with the rightist development strategy until the cultural revolution, when a significant spell of starry-eyed idealism started. But it had not much to do with the economic content but the aspects that she now lumped under the "ingrained Confucian respect for hierarchy". She stated that the principle of "to each according to his work" did not violate socialist morality, and the reintroduction of bonuses abolished during the cultural revolution was not a way of instituting incentives wages but were "evidently to be token awards to restore and reinforce the discipline of criticism and praise among peers which broke down wherever ultra-left influences prevailed" (Robinson, 1978a, 5).

Second, the use of profits as a criterion for efficient use of inputs did not amount to taking the capitalist road, so long as the prices were exogenously given and profits were handed over to the central planners for balanced investment. Joan Robinson had always made a distinction between profit as an index of efficiency and profit as a motive, but had also understood the Maoist position to be that the former necessarily leads to the latter (Robinson, 1969, 12–13). Now she found the Chinese position closer to hers:

> Profit—the excess of the annual value of output over costs—is mainly a reflection of economical and efficient use of materials (including sources of energy). Why should this be regarded as 'taking the capitalist road'? If the purpose of production is 'to serve the people' surely the more efficiently it is carried out the better its purpose is served. (Robinson, 1978a, 4–5)

Third, the removal of the revolutionary committees from industrial and commercial enterprises was good for the enterprises. As was noted above, even under the revolutionary committees, the rightist had managed to make the director personally responsible for failure. Small wonder that in some enterprises "the change from chairman of the revolutionary committee to director is only a change of name". In the case of "others, the imposition of a second layer of talk and argument between the Party committee and the executive reduced efficiency without guaranteeing democracy" (*ibid.*, 5–6). Fourth, on the questions of education and intellectuals, Robinson now agreed that "bullying intellectuals destroys their utility and now the immediate need is to restore their self-confidence".[10] She was, however, still concerned about "the natural tendency of education to provide the basis for the promotion of a new class". There was "ample scope" for it in the Chinese tradition. Besides this Confucian tradition, she also worried about the tradition of cramming (*ibid.*, 6–7).

Finally, and most seriously, she was sceptical about the new policy of modernisation, especially the capital-using bias of modern Western technology. She stated, however: "We know only too well what it is like to be modem. But it is foolish to judge policy merely from slogans" (*ibid.*, 4, 6). In an unpublished note, she analysed "modernisation of industry" in terms of her approach to the choice of technique, which she had outlined in her lectures in China in 1957. She believed that political economy needed a major innovation to show how the highly modern equipment resulting from fiercely competitive battles could be employed in what she regarded as humane relations of production in China to avoid the degrading labour process such as illustrated by Braverman (1974). China would have to learn to choose equipment in terms of output per unit of investment, and not in terms of output per worker to be employed. The equipment may be on offer not because China needs it to raise productivity, but because corporations have surpluses to invest (JVR Collection, ii/28.1. King's College).

On the whole, Joan Robinson was able to accept the major part of the post-Mao reform because she had had no serious problems with the rightist economic policies and management even in the past.[11] Her new theory about the anti-Confucian content of the cultural revolution was not only vague, but also somewhat hard to understand, as the movement to criticise Confucius in China was mainly directed against the commonsense pragmatism of Chou En-lai.

To her initial satisfaction, the reform focused on industry and education, with no significant change in the commune system. "In the work-point system in the communes, which organise the employment of three-quarters of the national labour force, the principle of reward for work was established from the first" (Robinson, 1978a, 4). This testifies to the view here that Joan Robinson had consistently taken a rightist stand on the question of work incentives in the Chinese agriculture. According to her, "Mao did not foresee what the greatest success of his policies was going to be." Having survived the first dose of post-Mao reform, she had now no doubt in her mind that her views about communes had been vindicated and that the self-managed commune was the most successful of all policies. Mao himself was considered to be dogmatic for the first time:

> There is one question on which Mao's open-mindedness seems to have been limited by dogma, that is the doctrine of the superiority of ownership of means of production 'by the whole people' over ownership by collective units such as co-operatives. Ownership by the whole people entails the control of production by bureaucracy and the overall allocation of output between consumption and accumulation by central decree.

> The doctrine is still maintained in China in theory but it is now recognised that the transition from the collective to state ownership, especially in agriculture, will take a very long time. Meanwhile, the experience of the communes is proving that self-management is compatible with a high rate of voluntary accumulation and not incompatible with a sufficient degree of central planning of the flows of output. (Robinson, 1979b, 53)

In a sense, Joan Robinson was back to the question raised during her 1957 lectures in China regarding the bureaucratic tendency in a planning system and her interest in a cooperative solution aroused during the cultural revolution. According to her, Mao's belief—"[i]f Marxist-Leninists are in control, the rights of the vast majority will be granted"—begged the "ancient question: Who controls the controllers?" (Robinson, 1978b, 27). The commune system, she thought, showed the direction towards a blend of cooperation and central planning. Even earlier, the point had been made that cooperatives required "the framework of a government policy genuinely directed to the interests of the peasantry" (Robinson and Eatwell, 1973, 325). Her *Aspects of Development and Underdevelopment* also came out around this time, which held out China as a successful model of development, particularly in agriculture.[12] She wrote:

> At a few points, I refer to Chinese experience by way of contrast with that of the Third World. China is a controversial subject, more than ever in 1978, but I do not think that anyone would deny that the Chinese method of organising a highly labour-intensive agriculture is more successful than any in the so-called free world. (Robinson, 1979a, Foreword)

By successful she meant a method that improved production as well as welfare of peasants: a system "which permits the cultivators to benefit themselves while supplying the needs of the economy" (*ibid.*, 58–9). Soon after quoting approvingly Jerome Ch'en's[13] "sarcastic" comment—China does not exist "to satisfy the ideological cravings of a handful of well- or ill-wishers" (Robinson, 1979c, 26), she had to admit: "Friends and admirers of the People's Republic are often perplexed and distressed at the news nowadays coming out of China" (Robinson, 1980, last page). The Chinese had speedily moved to de-collectivise agriculture.[14] In the reprint of her "little book" on development appeared the admission for the first time that her view of the Chinese agriculture was not flawless:

> News which has come out of China since the death of Mao shows that some of the allusions in what follows to the success of the Chinese agriculture were over optimistic; all the same, the level of production and the standard of nutrition compare favourably with those of the Third World. (Robinson, 1981, x)

China was thus to be judged by the ordinary indicators of development[15] and not from the perspective of leading the world in demonstrating that a cooperative solution, which would avoid the inequality of a competitive solution as well as the bureaucracy and elitism of a planning solution, was possible. Even by ordinary standards, average grain yield per hectare in China in 1979 was below South Korea and Taiwan, average growth rate of grain yields between 1955 and 1979 was below one-third of developing countries, and total factor productivity growth during 1959–79 was negative, suggesting organisational and managerial problems rather than a deficiency of critical inputs.[16] It must be remembered here that total factor productivity cannot allow for the enormous human costs imposed on the Chinese agriculture. These considerations allow Adelman and Sunding to conclude that collectivisation "may well have been more of a liability than an asset in productivity terms". But they also find "that China was and remains one of the developing countries with the most equal distribution of income" (1989, 716–18). This was despite the inter-commune inequality arising from what Robinson called "socialist rent", noted from the first and re-emphasised in her last writings as follows:

> Communes which enjoy the most natural conditions have the largest quotas and the highest money incomes. Their members can enjoy a better standard of life than those of the poorer communes, while at the same time carrying out more investment to increase their differential advantage in the future. A problem thus emerges for the authorities of how to check the growth of inequality without interfering with the growth of productivity. However, a floor has been set under the standard of life everywhere, so that

> this kind of inequality is not so distressing as inequality between those families that have something to eat and those who have not. (Robinson, 1979a, 1981, 58–9)

This means that the inter-commune inequality was not allowed to adversely influence the condition of the poor. Adelman and Sunding however note that while rural income distribution deteriorated after de-collectivisation, the rate of poverty reduction significantly improved (1989, 719). Not only that the poverty floor mentioned by Joan Robinson was very low,[17] it was based on local poverty relief and not on a well-thought-out policy which took account of very serious spatial differences (Nolan, 1988, 68–88).

Her last writing on China opened with the frankest admission: "I have been accused of being starry-eyed about the revolution and I have to admit some truth in the accusation."[18] The impact that the first visit had made on her had been "overwhelming", but one cannot fail to notice a pragmatic view of economic development in the *Letters*, and later in *Economic Perspective*. Ever since she had been "fighting off disillusionment until I could no longer accept the obscurantism, the violence and the downright silliness of the last stages of the Cultural Revolution".[19] Now she had to repudiate *Economic Management* also, saying: "I don't know if what I wrote was correct" (Robinson, 1982, 3).[20]

She was unsure even at the time of writing, as is evident from the following paragraph, which was deleted from the original draft of the foreword at the suggestion of Adler:

> To avoid tedious qualifications, I have written these notes in a positive style, but each statement should be taken with the proviso: 'this is what I was told, or rather: This is what I understood from what I was told. (JVR Collection, i1/15.5. King's College, Cambridge)

On the economy, the original draft concluded as under:

> In any case, for the time being at least, Chinese economic policy appears to be working better than any other planned economy, let alone the so-called developing countries in the toils of the world market. (JVR Collection, i/15.5)

In the final draft that was printed, the above conclusion was replaced by the impression that "the people whom one meets in China always seem much less nervous and ill-tempered than we are" (Robinson, 1973, 14).

Though disillusioned, Joan Robinson was still not cynical: "Whatever illusions I may have had, I feel that the reaction has gone too far. It is absurd to talk of ten wasted years (1966–76) for a great deal of construction went on in that period."[21] As she finally saw "it, whatever relapse there may be from the ideals of socialism, it will not be a relapse to the misery of old China" (Robinson, 1982, 3).

Joan Robinson's Insights and the Rightist Development Initiatives

What is there to salvage out of the work spread over three decades, repudiate as she did most of her known writings? Out of a lost vision emerged a consciousness of the real economic predicament. A number of ideas survived self-destruction as well as the turn of events. The first had been reiterated in the debate on "China since Mao": "How can any investment for development be made except out of 'surplus labour'? Whether it is best done directly or via exports to pay for imports is a matter for practical judgement" (Robinson, 1979c, 25). In revising her view of the Leap and the cultural revolution, she did not forget the tremendous construction or investment in these periods. The belief in high investment requiring a high rate of exploitation continued, despite the arguments against. Second, in her very first direct reference to China, she had predicted that the future of socialist development depended on its ability to deal with the growth of population (Robinson, 1949, 64). This view she never changed, although she was not always well-informed about the seriousness of the population policy in China. For instance, she still thought that the barefoot doctors "incidentally contributed a great deal, though not quite enough, to birth control" (Robinson, 1980, last page). Anyhow, the problem was stated as follows:

> One important change is that the new leadership has woken up to the fact that the population of China is already much higher than is convenient from a strategic, economic and political point of view and is still growing. Strategically, it is a weakness to have to import food. The more investment has to go into creating cultivable land, in the heroic manner of Dazhai or in large-scale river control schemes, the less is available for raising standards of consumption and reducing toil. 'Modernisation' more readily raises output per man, saving labour, than output per hectare, saving land. Politically, a conflict of interest between city and countryside is more immediate than class war in the usual sense. (Robinson, 1980, last page)

Population growth, though restrained over the seventies, had held back economic growth, especially in the rural sector. According to her, "[T]here is still a long way to go. The main advance in population control will have to be in the countryside, and it is here that the real difficulties lie." Not only that the population pressure had caused difficulties for economic growth, it had also caused physical setbacks. Thus "the floods in the Yangzi valley in 1981 were due to the tree cover of the valleys and foothills along the river being destroyed around the villages faster than it can be replanted" (Robinson, 1982, 3).[22] In the same vein was her emphasis on observing "limitations on the possibilities of growth. What the Chinese found when they started on the wild rush for modernisation was, for instance, that it is wasteful to build factories ahead of the availability of energy to operate them" (Robinson, 1979c, 25). Most interestingly, population growth was mentioned as "an important element in the relapse from egalitarian socialist ideals". It was unrealistic to expect the relatively better-off urban population and the educated segments "to wait for a rise in their own level of consumption till the great mass of the peasant families have been raised to the level the town families are now at" (Robinson, 1982, 3). Talking about class conflict "overlooks the main conflict of interests that the authorities have to try to reconcile—that between town and country" (Robinson, 1979c, 25).[23]

In the last phase, the conclusions arrived at on the basis of inadequate, even faulty, information and the value judgements about cooperative ideals seem to give way to the respect she had always felt for hard economic policy in a backward overpopulated economy. This was demonstrated by her broad and uncynical acceptance of the clearly rightist policy initiatives in China since Mao.

Notes

1. Robinson (1976a, 92).
2. Her uneasiness seems to have started with the news of the Lin Piao affair. Writing now for the *Spectator*, she conceded: "Knowing the language, of course, is an enormous benefit to the traveller, but it does not make very much difference to what he is able to report, for everyone he comes across is exceedingly discreet with a foreigner. For instance, soon after the death of Lin Piao, there was no one in China who had not heard of the official explanation of what had happened, but the resident foreigners never could get a word about it from their Chinese colleagues and friends" (Robinson, 1972, 321) But see also Robinson (1975b, 217), where she disputes the suggestion that, contrary to the official story, Lin had no ultra-left links.
3. Robinson (1954, 1975a).
4. Robinson (1954) and Robinson and Adler (1958).
5. There was no change in her view of the North Korean "economic miracle". See Robinson (1976a, 92, 1977b).
6. Watson's description of the book as a "superficial survey" had invited a sharp reaction from her. See Watson (1969, 164, 1970) and Robinson (1970, 4).
7. Beitelheim (1974).
8. See Robinson (1964c).
9. Ironically, Han Suyin's review of *The Cultural Revolution* had noted: "She shows that a personal struggle for succession such as followed the passing of Lenin and Stalin is being made impossible by the Cultural Revolution" (1969, last page).
10. This Joan Robinson was different from the one who, during the euphoria of the cultural revolution, had advised Samuelson "pointedly that it would be good for sedentary professors to lead a more active life in countryside". See Feiwel (1989, 136). Later she also talked of "the dreadful story of obscurantist persecution of scientists, which destroyed much valuable work and ruined many valuable lives" (Robinson, 1980, last page).

11. Griffin and Gurley (1985, 1135) note that Joan Robinson "questioned most of Bettelheim's interpretations of new policies, alleging either that the policies are not really new or that they are not incompatible with the pursuit of socialism".
12. According to one reviewer, Joan Robinson's "pro-Chinese bias is prevalent throughout the book sometimes even at the cost of objectivity" (Dhesi, 1981, 668). Bruton (1981, 195) accused her "of resolving all puzzles with a call for rational planning or a reference to China". Bronfenbrenner (1980, 1582) remarked that it was written "with one eye cocked on China". Helleiner was dismissive: "One cannot honestly recommend it—not even to intelligent radical friends" (1980, 517).
13. See Ch'en (1969).
14. See Nolan (1983a, b, 1988).
15. In the days of cultural revolutionary fervour, Joan Robinson did not think that the Chinese "suffer from not waving their flag of national income" (Robinson, 1968, 691–2).
16. In fact, the growth of inputs had been rapid. However, for the growth of output, "the system needed a lot of capital" (Nolan, 1988, 54).
17. According to White (1989): "[W]hat must have exacerbated the conflict [during the cultural revolution] was that in China the economic pie had to be tranched in such small wedges."
18. After noting that Joan Robinson "was never the one to accept being told what to believe", one obituary went as far as to claim that disillusionment with China may have been a cause of her death: "Joan Robinson was undoubtedly shaken by discovering that she had failed, like everyone else, to understand that China, even in a cultural revolution, presents a carefully laundered face to foreigners, however friendly. It was thus possible for the enemies of China and of socialism to criticise Joan Robinson's work for SACU in a way that she found difficult to refute. This surely depressed her and is likely to have been a cause of the severe stroke that effectively killed her" (Hart, 1983, 27).
19. She now knew more: "Too much broke loose in the process and there was conflict, even with guns, in many places" (Robinson, 1980, last page). For an interesting explanation of the causes of violence during the cultural revolution, see White (1989).
20. A commentator had wondered: "Her account makes a very seductive reading, for the picture it presents of the Chinese economy is one of remarkable harmony." See *China Quarterly* (1973, 799).

21. Raj (1983, 73) also takes the view that the communes permitted large-scale investment in agriculture. The impact of the post-Mao price incentives has to be seen in the perspective of the constraints relaxed by this investment. According to Lardy (1988, 256), per capita farm private investment in 1983 was less than its level during the period before the formation of cooperatives.
22. Earlier she had noted during the cultural revolution "a parallel movement to save the health of the terrain by afforestation and conservation, carried out by the same means of mass mobilisation as the campaign for healthy humanity" (Robinson, 1980, last page).
23. On the significance of the rural-urban issue, see Nolan (1979) and Nolan and White (1984).

References

Published Works

Adelman, I. and D. Sunding. (1989) 'Joan Robinson as a Development Economist,' in G.R. Feiwel (ed.), *Joan Robinson and Modern Economic Theory*, 702–22. London: Macmillan.

Beitelheim, C. (1974) *Cultural Revolution and Industrial Organisation in China*. New York: Monthly Review Press.

———. (1978a) 'Letter of Resignation to the Franco-Chinese Friendship Association,' *Monthly Review*, 30, 9–13.

———. (1978b) 'The Great Leap Backward,' *Monthly Review*, 30, 37–130.

Braverman, H. (1974) *Labor and Monopoly Capital*. New York: Monthly Review Press.

Bronfenbrenner, M. (1980) 'Review of Robinson (1979c),' *Journal of Economic Literature*, 18, 1581–2.

Bruton, H.J. (1981) 'Review of Robinson (1979b),' *Economic Development and Cultural Change*, 30, 191–6.

Ch'en, J. (1969) *Mao*. Englewood Cliffs, NJ: Prentice Hall.

China Quarterly (1973) 'Book Notes,' 56, 798–9.

Dhesi, A.S. (1981) 'Review of Robinson (1979c),' *Kyklos*, 34, 668–70.

Feiwel, G.R. (ed.). (1989) *Joan Robinson and Modern Economic Theory*. London: Macmillan.

Griffin, K. and J. Gurley. (1985) 'Radical Analyses of Imperialism, the Third World, and the Transition to Socialism: A Survey Article,' *Journal of Economic Literature*, 23, 1089–143.

Han Suyin. (1969) Review of Robinson (1969a). Broadsheet, 6, last page.

Hart, A.T. (1983) 'Joan Robinson: A Personal Note,' *China Now*, 107, 27.

Helleiner, G.K. (1980) 'Review of Robinson (1979b),' *Canadian Journal of Economics*, 3, 515–7.

Lardy, N.R. (1988) 'Comments on Deng Fureng,' in G. Ranis and T.P. Schultz (eds.), *The State of Development Economics*, 254–9. Oxford: Basil Blackwell.

Nolan, P. (1979) 'Inequality of Income between Town and Countryside in the People's Republic of China in the Mid-1950s,' *World Development*, 7, 447–65.

———. (1983a) 'De-collectivisation of Agriculture in China, 1979–82: A Long-term Perspective,' *Economic and Political Weekly*, 8(1395–1406), 1434–41.

———. (1983b) 'De-collectivisation of Agriculture in China,' *Cambridge Journal of Economics*, 7, 381–403.

———. (1988) *The Political Economy of Collective Farms: An Analysis of China's Post-Mao Reform*. Cambridge: Polity Press.

Nolan, P. and G. White. (1984) 'Urban Bias, Rural Bias or State Bias? Urban-rural Relations in Post-revolutionary China,' *Journal of Development Studies*, 20, 52–81.

Raj, K.N. (1983) 'Agricultural Growth in India and China,' *Economic and Political Weekly*, 18, 69–75.

Robinson, Joan. (1949) 'Theory of Planning,' Review of M. Dobb. *Soviet Economic Development Since 1917, Soviet Studies*, 1, 60–4.

———. (1954) *Letters from a Visitor to China*. Cambridge: Students' Bookshops.

———. (1964a) 'Notes from China,' *Economic Weekly*, 16, 195–203.

———. (1964b) 'A British Economist on Chinese Communes,' *Eastern Horizon*, 3, 6–11.

———. (1964c) 'The Chinese Point of View,' *International Affairs*, 40, 232–44.

———. (1965) 'What's New in China?' *Eastern Horizon*, 4, 11–5.

———. (1968) 'China Today: Economic Organisation,' *Journal of the Royal Society of Arts*, 116, 683–93.

———. (1969) *The Cultural Revolution in China*. Harmondsworth, Middlesex: Penguin Books.

———. (1970) 'Reply to A.J. Watson,' *China Now*, 2, 4.

———. (1972) 'Through Western Spectacles,' Reviews of K. Mehnert, *China Today*; Terrill (1972); and K. Ling, *Red Guard, Spectator*, 7522, 321.

———. (1973) *Economic Management in China, 1972*. London: Anglo-Chinese Educational Institute.
———. (1975a) 'National Minorities in Yunnan,' *Eastern Horizon*, 14, 32–43.
———. (1975b) 'The Fall of Lin Piao.' Review of P. Worsley, *Inside China*; K.S. Karol, *The Second Chinese Evolution, Spectator*, 7677, 217.
———. (1976a) 'Review of J.K. Fairbank, et al.,' *East Asia: Tradition and Transformation, Journal of Royal Asiatic Society* 76, 91–2.
———. (1976b) 'An Eyewitness Account of the Cultural Revolution,' Review of John and Elsie Collier, *China's Socialist Revolution, Monthly Review*, 28, 50–1.
———. (1977a) *Reports from China, 1953–76*. London: Anglo-Chinese Educational Institute.
———. (1977b) 'Review of E. Brun and J. Hersh. *Socialist Korea: A Case Study in the Strategy of Economic Development*,' *Monthly Review* 29, 60–2.
———. (1978a) 'China 1978: Comments on Bettelheim,' *China Now*, 80, 4–7.
———. (1978b) 'Review of Mao Tse-tung (1977),' *China Now*, 80, 26–7.
———. (1979a) *Aspects of Development and Underdevelopment*. Cambridge: Cambridge University Press.
———. (1979b) 'Review of MAO (1977),' *Monthly Review*, 30, 52–3.
———. (1979c) 'The Pros and Cons,' *China Now*, 86, 25–6.
———. (1980) Review of N. Maxwell (ed.) *China's Road to Development, Broadsheet*, 17, last page.
———. (1981) Reprint of Robinson (1979b).
———. (1982) 'Introduction,' *China Now*, 100, 3.
Robinson, Joan and S. Adler. (1958) *China: An Economic Perspective*. London: Fabian International Bureau, Fabian Tract No. 314.
Robinson, Joan and J. Eatwell. (1973) *An Introduction to Modern Economics*. London: McGraw-Hill.
Watson, A.J. (1969) 'Review of Robinson (1969a),' *China Quarterly*, 40, 163–4.
———. (1970) 'The Cultural Revolution: Two Views,' *China Now*, 2, 3–4.
White, L.T. (1989) *Politics of Chaos: The Organisational Causes of Violence in China's Cultural Revolution*. Princeton: Princeton University Press.

6

Concluding Observations

This volume started by surveying Joan Robinson's numerous but scattered writings on China, contributed over a period of nearly three decades (1953–82). These contributions were then divided into three phases, broadly reflecting important shifts of emphasis in her stance on the strategic issues in the development of China.

It was shown that in the first phase, lasting from 1953 until Joan Robinson's third visit and involving contributions based on her first two visits and news from China till 1963, she was largely on her own: enthusiastic and sympathetic, but at the giving rather than the receiving end of ideas. Unlike the Soviet Union on the eve of revolution, China was backward as well as overpopulated. Capital accumulation, being the key determinant of development and industrialisation according to Joan Robinson, had to be accelerated together with a strong family planning programme. Too much capital accumulation was to be avoided by a choice of technique based on the maximisation of output per unit of investment.[1] Consumers were thus to be treated better than in Eastern Europe. Central planning would overcome the unjust outcomes associated with the price system mainly by abolishing personal property, while the bureaucratisation characterising planning would be somewhat relaxed

P. Tahir, *Making Sense of Joan Robinson on China*, Palgrave Studies in the History of Economic Thought, https://doi.org/10.1007/978-3-030-28825-9_6

by not abolishing the prices and the market altogether and by *supplementing* material incentives with a moral code.

Agriculture existed to produce a surplus for industry: socialist organisation suited industry more than agriculture, "*because it is very difficult to organise labour in agriculture*".[2] Yet land reform was considered transitional for fear of demography beating the holding size and the contradictory fear of land sales, permissible at the time, bringing back the iniquitous structure of the past. Collectivisation was stated by Robinson to be necessary to forestall the restoration of an unequal distribution, besides further yield improvement, mechanisation and release of labour for industry. But Joan Robinson did not clearly support collectivisation until her second visit, as she was not yet certain as to how the Soviet mistakes would be avoided in China. During the second visit, she was informed that the cooperativisation in the mid-fifties had in general been voluntary and learned during irrigation work. Irrigation involves obvious externalities, but she still questioned the need for a larger size in the absence of significant mechanisation, as it complicated the problem of organising labour. In addition, cooperativisation dealt with the equity question quantitatively—there was no danger of demography or land sales causing a skewed land distribution—but not qualitatively. As income depended on procurement prices or prices in the small but lucrative private market, what she called "socialist rent", arising from differential soil fertility, choice of crops and locational advantages, would cause differentials in earnings per worker between cooperatives. Thus an issue of major concern in subsequent debates—inter-collective inequality—was identified from the first. Her solution, a land tax in money terms to fully mop up the differential, was never put into operation. The agricultural tax that existed was a mere symbol.[3] A differential arising mainly from the quality of property was thus allowed to persist in a socialist organisation.

Joan Robinson never dealt with intra-collective inequality. But there was a fair amount of discussion about the terms of trade between agriculture and industry. Until supply trailed behind demand, agricultural prices were supposed to be set below demand prices. Her proposed land tax would thus correspond to agricultural surplus, and the extent to which it covered government spending determined the burden to be imposed on industry, which in turn indicated the pattern of prices to be set for it.

Industrial enterprises were not to be allowed to determine their own prices not only to stop them from behaving capitalistically, but more importantly to allow the planners to apportion inter-sectoral burdens fairly and without prejudicing the incentive to work and produce.

Since prices were to be determined politically, keeping in view the requirements of a reasonable surplus for capital accumulation, Joan Robinson believed that there would neither be inflation nor unemployment in the socialist economy of China.

The interaction of the above views of Joan Robinson with the Chinese reality did not produce extreme tensions in the first phase. In the years after the revolution and the period of first five-year plan, China was not shy of providing economic information. Joan Robinson's accounts of these years, even the clean-and-honest image, were not significantly different from other accounts or the facts on the ground. The peasants' squeeze, workers' exploitation and the rate of accumulation were not disturbingly high. Nor could the achievement of price stability, high economic growth and improvements in health and nutrition be denied, when compared with the pre-1949 situations. On the questions of population, prices and the market under socialism and money rent, Joan Robinson was more enthusiastic than the Chinese. But who could deny the logic of these arguments? What was questionable was her view of a high rate of capital accumulation as the critical determinant of development and the absolute necessity of agricultural collectivisation.

Strangely enough, the group in the Chinese Communist Party that had been dubbed as the rightists by the time she arrived in China in 1957, and which were not very much unlike her, is not mentioned in her writings of the first phase. This group viewed China as a backward overpopulated economy requiring a sustained development of productive forces through central planning supplemented by a regulated use of prices and the market, is not mentioned in her writings of the first phase. She presented a monolithic view of Chinese political economy. As the five-antis campaign was clearly against the old bourgeoisie, it was touched on in the *Letters* but without any suggestion that it was the first campaign against the right wing of the party. (In fact, it was in organising transactions with these remnants of capitalism that the rightists devised a stabilising role for the internal trade ministry extolled by Joan Robinson in all phases of her China connection.) Similarly in the second half of the fifties, there is no discussion of the "hundred flowers movement" and the following campaign against the rightists. Either Robinson could not understand the basis of the existence of the rightists even after the high tide of socialism, incidentally ignored completely in the main text of *Economic Perspective* and referred to only in a postscript made necessary by the news of the Leap, or she did not dispute their stand. The latter seems more plausible because at that time, based in England, she did not envisage the Leap as altering the basic pattern of the Chinese economy.

The radical trappings of Joan Robinson began only after the Sino-Soviet conflict, on which she was given the Chinese brief during the third and fourth visits, but a real transformation had to await the fifth visit—her pilgrimage to China of the cultural revolution.[4] After the Leap in 1958, China stopped publishing statistics altogether. Instead of informing the world about the true nature of developments taking place in China so as to discourage distorted writings by the ill-informed, she indulged during the second phase (roughly 1964–75) in what can only be described as a hagiographic stance. Thus the massive famine never happened. Rather it could not have happened with the invention of the commune system. The difficulties and errors were all recognised—the need-based distribution and communal eating, the attack on the family and its plots, the large-scale transfer of labour to nonagricultural pursuits such as steelmaking and to irrigation and other collective activities.

All these difficulties were, however, seen as the necessary costs of an enormous learning-by-doing experiment. It is clear from all accounts that Joan Robinson did not know about the famine; she did not hide anything that she knew but she did fail to assess the possibility of enormous errors like the famine in enormous experiments such as the Leap and the commune movement. When she herself arrived in China in 1963, the rightists led by Liu had effectively reduced the commune size to what used to be lower-form cooperatives, curtailed the nonagricultural roles, restored distribution according to work and reactivated some private activity. Family planning was heard of again. On the whole, by ending the uncertainty created by the various campaigns of the Leap and restoring material incentives in agriculture and industry, the rightists had carried out a strict economic adjustment programme. So what she saw in the third visit could not have looked significantly different from what she had known in the second visit. And a rightist administration which, as opposed to the Maoists, admitted policy errors together with natural calamities being responsible for the disasters of the Leap kept her in the dark about the famine.[5]

Nevertheless, it is not incorrect to say that ever since the beginning of the China connection, Joan Robinson had been the victim of a self-delusion. She always believed that underneath the Chinese ideological verbiage existed an unfailing sense of economics as the art of the possible. Variously she described it as trial and error, scientific method and social experimentation. She was impressed by what she described as the Chinese way of pushing policies and programmes to the limit and then withdrawing while learning from the mistakes made during practice (Robinson, 1970a, 4). There was "a central line of development" which tenaciously survived the right-left struggles (Robinson, 1974d). Even after her only visit to China since Mao she admitted that she "was relying too much on what I have always felt was a remarkable instinct for economic management of the Chinese administration" (Robinson, 1979f, 25). This volume has argued that this central line or sensible economic management approvingly cited by Joan Robinson was directly associated with the rightist influence, invariably in evidence whenever the Maoists failed in their superhuman campaigns to jump over "the China Walls" of economic and social backwardness.

Her first four visits coincided with the rightist economic regimes, confirming to her the recovery of the Chinese economy from the five-antis campaign, the socialist high tide and the Great Leap. The fifth visit, which was undertaken to study the cultural revolution, was the first when she got the feel of an actual Maoist campaign and its militant opposition to the right. If the Great Leap was a macro experiment involving the whole economy, the cultural revolution was first practised at a micro level at Dazhai brigade, in what she considered to be a pilot project to retry the abandoned principles of the Leap. During the cultural revolution, she had thought that the Dazhai's own bootstraps strategy might be a way around the persistent inter-commune inequality. Later on in her visit culminating in the writing of *Economic Management,* she would observe the return even of the Dazhai brigade to the central line in agriculture. The problem of inter-commune inequality also persisted.

Agriculture, at any rate, was largely unaffected by the ideas of the cultural revolution, which focused essentially on education and industry. While property differentials arising from socialist rent caused inter-commune inequality, access to education led to intellectual property differentials. The impact of these differentials was most keenly felt in industrial management. Moral incentives, serve the people, putting politics in command and democratic management were all slogans giving expression to the Maoist egalitarianism and in which Joan Robinson was deeply embedded during the cultural revolution. However, as noted above, the visit to China in connection with the cultural revolution was the first when she could be described as an eyewitness to a Maoist campaign.

Based on the ideals of the cultural revolution, she could for the first time feel that the inequality of a decentralised market economy and the bureaucracy of a centralised planned economy were after all not necessary evils. Perhaps she also got wind of the power struggle being staged under the banner of the cultural revolution. That must be why she was "fighting off disillusionment" (Robinson, 1982, 3) for some time and at some point even gave up on the cultural revolution experiment to return to the common-sense rightist principles of *Economic Management*. Thus when post-Mao reforms were put into operation, she had no serious problems with the attempts to put the profit back in command and the restoration of material incentives. As opposed to Bettelheim's view that China was taking a Great Leap Backward, she believed it to be the triumph of the common-sense economic policy and management—until China since Mao took a different view of the rate of investment[6] and agricultural collectivisation.

Even after seeing the problems created by the Great Leap and the cultural revolution, Joan Robinson would not disregard the benefits of high investments made during these years. This goes against her critiques of the Stalinist strategy of high-handed industrialisation and the Dobb-Sen technique, as well as her perception that the Chinese industrialisation respected consumer sovereignty rather than promoting producer initiative. She had hit the nail on the head when she observed in the case of Czechoslovakia: "When the rate of growth slackened and actually came to a halt, the authorities could think of no remedy except more investment"

(Robinson, 1967h, 36–7). In China as well, excessive investment rates were associated with negative growth (Dong, 1982, 90–1).

During 1952–57, Burma and China had the same average rates of investment, while Taiwan trailed behind both (Yeh, 1968, 513–5). It is obviously hazardous to base any conclusions about economic development on high rates of investment. Managerial resources, for which the cultural revolution cultivated a distaste, need to be accumulated as speedily as fixed capital.[7] Until she was mesmerised by the communes, Joan Robinson believed that "[s]ocialism is very much better fitted to industry than to agriculture" (Robinson, 1963a, 9). Her main explanation—the peculiar difficulties of organising labour in agriculture on a large scale—has been cited as "the main explanation of the abundant evidence" about the inverse relationship between output per unit of land and the farm size (Ellman, 1981, 982).[8] Joan Robinson did not agree with Mao's view of the communes as a temporary stage in the ultimate collectivisation in the form of state farms. She thought that since the Leap, the rightists had solved the problem of labour deployment by arriving at an appropriately reduced size of the team. In addition, the serve-the-people ideology had blended individual incentive with collective advantage. In fact she argued that the Chinese agriculture had become more labour intensive after collectivisation and that the increased value of workpoints increased the supply of effort. The de-collectivisation process initiated by the post-Mao reformers came to her as a surprise. However, her argument about the absence of a perverse backward bend in the supply of effort has been found to be problematic.[9]

In the last writing on China (Robinson, 1982), Joan Robinson underscored the fact that the communes had ensured that there would be no relapse to the increasing misery of pre-revolution rural China[10] At the same time, the post-Mao relapse from egalitarian ideals suggested to her that the end of rural misery had not brought about any significant reduction in the rural-urban gap.[11] It is a startling outcome, given the fact that the rural teams retained per capita increases of output while per capita increase of industrial output was rarely passed on in wages (Government of Pakistan, 1975, 26). In other words, the Maoist emphasis on egalitarianism kept agricultural growth lower than it could have been. The high growth of rural relative to urban population was given as the main explanation. The Maoists were never serious about population control and the commune system. By discouraging outmigration, they made the demographic distribution worse. In addition, food security worked as an incentive for higher dependency ratios.[12] There was too much labour to be supervised. If the "managers" could demonstrate the uninterrupted delivery of minimum needs and a rising investment, they were seen to have "efficiently" served the local as well as the whole people. Repeatedly, Joan Robinson made the sweeping statement that China had no problem of unemployment,[13] neglecting the existence of a serious underemployment problem, as the collectives were not supposed to dismiss workers, besides seeking to maximise income per man-year rather than return per unit of work (Robinson, 1967b, 222). The restrictions on migration made the situation worse.

While the arguments for collectivisation based essentially on presumptions regarding self-motivation[14] become suspect once the non-existence of these presumptions becomes clear, the arguments derived from the need to carry out projects involving substantial externalities were never the arguments for collectivisation per se. Sound theoretical arguments have existed for cooperation in many services to agriculture even before the advent of the communes. However, so far as Joan Robinson is concerned, "the issue is never faced whether it is optimal to suppress hierarchy, private ownership and group honour—if the desire for them is deeply engrained—or to accept them while trying to remove their external diseconomies" (Whitehead, 1971, 80).

Thus, Joan Robinson's problems vis-à-vis China may not have been informational alone. First, she looked for a planning solution with a regulated market for high growth. Then she was lured away by the egalitarian hopes of a cooperative solution. The main burden of evidence now available shows that China did manage to achieve a bit of both. It also shows that China continues to be a backward overpopulated economy: its industrialisation experiment produced results that were nowhere near Robinson's prediction that it would be as important in the second half of the twentieth century as that of the United States in the second half of the nineteenth century (Robinson, 1954b). The succession of various mass campaigns, aimed according to her to educate the Chinese to avoid becoming "selfish and corrupt" like the Westerners when they "become rich like them" (Robinson, 1975c, 46), seems, therefore, to have been well before the event.

Her fascination with a paternal, socialist state goes back to the thirties: "[F]ew children would freely spend on education as much as their parents think right, and if the parents may coerce the children, it is difficult to argue that the state ought not to coerce the parents" (Robinson, 1937, 290).[15] But in the early thinking of Joan Robinson, the presumption in favour of the state was not necessarily a prejudice against the capitalists. This came much later, with a Keynesian interpretation of the *rentier* aspect of capitalism, and as part of what appears to have been a long but elusive search for her: a socioeconomic organisation that could extract the desired surplus without letting it dissipate into the capitalist consumption on the one hand and without having to depress the already poor consumption of the workers on the other; an organisation, so to speak, to do the job of capitalism—exploitation.[16] In her very first writing, Joan Robinson had been worried that public control would lead to capital outflow. Later, she analysed the rentier state in some detail, only to repeat the old fear about capital flight (Robinson, 1930, 296, 1966h, 67–70).

The objection was not to the rentier or the capitalist function; the state had to intervene to perform these functions. Such being the case in developed structures, which she had in view in both of the aforementioned writings, the situation in the underdeveloped structures would be far worse, leading her to conclude that the state had to assume the function of the capitalist. "It is true that the rich save more than the poor, but do they not also consume more" (Robinson, 1980a, 131). But does not the state consume and waste even more? She took some note of it, too, in her criticism of the "warfare state", devoted to defence at the expense of development, "which increases poverty rather than relieving it" (Robinson, 1976c, 9). Similarly, the early emphasis on fixed industrial capital formation seems to have been somewhat reconsidered later (Robinson, 1974b, 221).

The readiness to reconsider is a reflection of the sense of the practical in her work on development, with theory serving only to clarify logical arguments. This sense of development as the art of the possible, for instance, led her to advise a socialist government in Sri Lanka against nationalising the efficiently run tea plantations under foreign ownership.

In the same vein, she told the Pakistanis—who considered having a steel mill to be the *sine qua non* of national economic independence—to develop through trade (Robinson, 1959, 1964i). The point being made here becomes clear from the menu of teaching suggested by Joan Robinson for the students from developing countries. It was important to teach "analysis, not doctrine". Though the "Keynesian revolution finally shattered the presumption in favour of laissez-faire", Joan Robinson thought it was "just as important to warn our pupils against new bad mental habits as against the old ones". She went on to give some remarkable examples, starting with the "insufficiently disaggregated" second plan of India: "In particular, global thinking leads to overlooking the differences in treatment required for agriculture and industry." Second, "the purchasing power of foreign exchange over equipment and know-how for investment is far higher than the purchasing power of home resources". Third, "we must not lose sight of what was valuable in the old orthodoxy. In the U.S.S.R. the laws of supply and demand had to be learned the hard way." Fourthly, the "law of comparative costs must not be forgotten when the development of new export industries is being discussed" (Robinson, 1967j, 49–50).

A stream that runs through her writings is to keep the analysis separate from ideology: "Analysis that is put at the service of ideology is not interesting" (Robinson, 1973b, 261). It is well-nigh impossible to label her. She can be quoted against any label—communist, Marxist, neo-Marxist, structuralist, dependency theorist. However, material can also be found in her writings nearly under all of these labels. If Shove (1933, 657) found her first major book "surprisingly … conservative" for the young author that she was at the time, *Business Week* saw her as a "socialist who sounds like a conservative".[17]

Her writings on China, as this volume has shown, provide an exception. For a large part, they leave an indomitable impression that some vague ideology commands analysis. More or less, her presumptions in favour of capital accumulation and the state, the prejudice against capitalism and her sense of development as the art of the possible are reflected in her stories about China. The main finding here is that the essential core of her economic interpretations consisted of a set of propositions not significantly different from those held by the so-called rightists in Mao's China. During the cultural revolution she nursed the illusion of a cooperative arrangement motivated by service rather than profit, which would overcome not only the bureaucratic tendency of central planning but also the injustice associated with the market system. Ever since she had been fighting off disillusionment until the rightist takeover in the later half of the seventies, in whose policy goals she found a broad reaffirmation of the policy set she had stood for before the cultural revolution and which she quickly recovered as more reliable information confirmed that the cultural revolution was more a struggle for power and not the social experiment she believed it to be. But since she held back the expression of disillusionment as it occurred, and wrote optimistic accounts based on inadequate and distorted information, many of her writings did not make sense even to friends in the economics profession.

In general, her own attitude at the end of most analyses was to leave the conclusion to the reader or to utilise the space to warn the reader as to what the analysis was not about.[18] Thus she was like literary critics who cannot compose poetry themselves. The sympathetic critics applaud her for a "good demolition job" but point all the same to the absence of an alternative theory.[19] Economic development was only one of her concerns. Interestingly, Harcourt (1984, 652) notes the same type of criticism against her main theoretical work. It appears that while the analyses by her were critiques mainly of capitalist and, to some extent, Soviet-type development, for an alternative she looked towards China, in whose case she justified more than she analysed. Her demolition work may be said to have been demolished with government after government failing to do the job of capitalism.

Notes

1. Even her further elaboration of this technique later (Robinson, 1977a) left open the question of how it would work in a real-life micro-setting. However, Wuyts (1981) has worked out interesting applications of the technique for the Mozambican agriculture.
2. Emphasis added. See Robinson (1963a, 9).

3. With a contribution of only 10 per cent of national income, "it might be argued that all this fuss and complication is not worthwhile [but] delivering the tax grain after the harvest has become symbolic" (Robinson, 1973f, 12).
4. Caute (1977, 376) describes Joan Robinson's *The Cultural Revolution* as "a short book which combined gullibility with latent authoritarianism in doses which were virtually standard among fellow-travellers of a certain camp".
5. Indeed a "brick wall of silence" about the famine has been maintained even after the return of the rightists in the post-Mao period. See Wright (1989a, b, 3).
6. See *Social Sciences in China* (March 1982, 25–6).
7. As Kerr et al. put it (1973, 35, 147, 282), "Dams, power plants and factories can be built in a few years, but it may take decades to develop domestically the engineers, scientists, administrators, and managers to operate them." These authors would also question another of Joan Robinson's arguments for socialism—its ability to quickly dismantle precapitalist cultures—by finding no significant evidence for them to be "serious impediments to economic development". Indeed, the early fears about the precapitalist cultures inhibiting entrepreneurial development have been belied by experience. See Leff (1979).
8. See also Nolan (1988, 42–3).
9. Joan Robinson's case rested on the assumption that shirking is kept in check by mutual pressure to prevent a slowdown in the rise of the value of workpoints. Macrae (1977, 379–80) thinks it is not so because a shirker if detected would be awarded lower workpoints anyway. The real problem is the detection of shirking in the conditions of team production. See also Liu Minquan (1989, 1990).
10. The famine during the commune movement, however, was massive even by pre-1949 standards and the communes played a role in causing it. See Brammall (1989) and Riskin (1987).
11. Although Joan Robinson devoted her seventh visit to China undertaken in 1975 to the study of minority regions, she did not pay much attention to the regional dimension of inequality. The problem had been aggravated by the autarkic policies of the communes.
12. The high rural population growth also puts in doubt her many statements about the equality of the sexes. Nolan and White report "the tendency for women to receive systematically less work points, [e]ven in Dazhai" (1979, 30).

13. See *China Quarterly*, No. 56, 759.
14. Continuous self-motivation requires continuous cultural revolution (Ishikawa, 1975, 447). Whatever information exists about the costs of one cultural revolution makes it non-repeatable.
15. The fact of the matter is that the struggle for expenditure allocation in the arena of developmental states by various class interests is more likely to lead to a very small share for education, especially primary education; higher education is represented as an interest in the state allocation process.
16. She chose the pages of a development journal, and a special issue to honour a pioneering development economist, to say, "Those who do not like to describe this as exploitation should provide another name for it" (Robinson, 1979c, 693).
17. 20 October 1975. On the one hand she considered the notion of equilibrium inappropriate in the context of economic development (Robinson, 1963b, 300; Seers, 1963, 1979) and, on the other hand, she criticised the structuralist approaches of Chenery and others (Robinson, 1980a, 132).
18. See, for instance, the conclusion of her major work: Robinson (1956a).
19. *Journal of Contemporary Asia* (1983, 3–4).

References

Unpublished Material

Brammall, C.M. (1989) Inequality and Poverty in Rural China: The Case of Sichuan Province, 1931–1978. Unpublished PhD dissertation, University of Cambridge.

Published Works

Caute, D. (1977) *The Fellow-travellers*. London: Quartet Books.

Dong, F. (1982) 'Relationship between Accumulation and Consumption,' in Xu Dixin, et al. (eds.), *China's Search for Economic Growth*. Beijing: New World Press.

Ellman, M. (1981) 'Agricultural Productivity under Socialism,' *World Development*, 9, 979–89.
Government of Pakistan (1975) *Economic and Manpower Planning in People's Republic of China: Report of the Delegation of Development Planners and Manpower Experts to People's Republic of China*. Islamabad: Printing Corporation of Pakistan.
Harcourt, G.C. (1984) 'Harcourt on Robinson,' in H.W. Speigel and W.J. Samuels (eds.), *Contemporary Economists in Perspective*, Vol. 1, Part B. London: Jai Press, 639–54.
Ishikawa, S. (1975) 'The Chinese Method of Technological Development: The Case of Agricultural Machinery and Implement Industry,' *Developing Economies*, 13, 430–58.
Journal of Contemporary Asia. (1983) Editorial 3, 3–6.
Kerr, C., et al. (1973) *Industrialism and Industrial Man*. Harmondsworth, Middlesex: Penguin.
Leff, N. (1979) 'Entrepreneurship and Economic Development: The Problem Revisited,' *Journal of Economic Literature*, 7, 46–64.
Liu Minquan. (1989) *Work Incentives in the Production Team in Southern Jiangsu, China, 1960s–70s*. Ld'A-QEH Development Studies Working Paper No. 10, University of Oxford.
———. (1990) *Incentives and Labour Under the Communes in China*. In progress PhD dissertation, University of Oxford.
Macrae, J. (1977) 'Production, Distribution and Economic Organisation: Income Distribution and Resource Allocation at the Team Level in Rural China,' *Journal of Development Economics*, 4, 365–85.
Nolan, P. (1988) *The Political Economy of Collective Farms: An Analysis of China's Post-Mao Reform*. Cambridge: Polity Press.
Nolan, P. and G. White. (1979) 'Socialist Development and Rural Inequality: The Chinese Countryside in the Seventies,' *Journal of Peasant Studies*, 7, 3–48.
Riskin, C. (1987) *China's Political Economy: The Quest for Development Since 1949*. New York: Oxford University Press.
Robinson, Joan. (1930) 'Review of H. CLAY *The Problem of Industrial Relations*,' *Political Quarterly*, 1, 293–6.
———. (1937) 'Review of R.H. HALL, *The Economic System in a Socialist State*,' *Cambridge Review*, 58, 289–90.
———. (1954b) 'Britain and China,' *Nation*, 179, 125–8.
———. (1956a) *The Accumulation of Capital* 1st ed. London: Macmillan.

———. (1959) 'Economic Possibilities of Ceylon,' in *Papers by Visiting Economists*, 38–71. Colombo: National Planning Council.
———. (1963a) 'Public and Private Enterprise,' *Applied Economic Papers*, 1–12.
———. (1963b) 'Review of G. Maynard,' *Economic Development and the Price Level, Economic Journal*, 73, 299–300.
———. (1964i) 'Planning for Economic Development,' *Trade Journal* (Pakistan), June–July, 5–7.
———. (1966h) *Economics: An Awkward Corner*. London: George Allen and Unwin.
———. (1967b) 'The Soviet Collective Farm as a Producer Cooperative: Comment,' *American Economic Review*, 57(1), 222–3.
———. (1967h) 'Socialist Affluence,' in C.H. Feinstein (ed.), *Socialism, Capitalism and Economic Growth: Essays in Honour of Maurice Dobb*. London: Cambridge University Press. Also in Robinson, (1973a), 33–47.
———. (1967j) 'Opening Remarks,' in K. Martin and John Knapp (eds.), *The Teaching of Development Economics*. London: Frank Cass, 149–50.
———. (1970a) 'Reply to A.J. Watson,' *China Now*, 2, 4.
———. (1973b) "Ideology and analysis"; a contribution to the Festschrift for Eduard Marz, Europaverlags A.G. Wien; in Robinson (1979a), 254–61.
———. (1973f) *Economic Management in China, 1972*. London: Anglo-Chinese Educational Institute.
———. (1974b) "Inflation West and East," *Frontier* (Calcutta) October 19, 215–21.
———. (1974d) 'Two Revolutions,' *Broadsheet*, 11, 4.
———. (1975c) *Economic Management in China*. 2nd ed. London: Anglo-Chinese Educational Institute.
———. (1976c) 'Introduction,' Kalecki, M. (1976) *Essays on Developing Economies*. Hassocks, Sussex: Harvester Press.
———. (1977a) 'Employment and the Choice of Technique,' in K.S. Krishnaswamy et al., (ed.) *Society and Change*. Bombay: Oxford University Press, 156–69.
———. (1979c) 'Surplus Value and Profits: The Rectification of Names,' *Development and Change*, 10, 693–5.
———. (1979f) 'The Pros and Cons,' *China Now*, 86, 25–6.
———. (1980a) 'Review of H. Chenery,' *Structural Change and Development Policy, Journal of Developing Areas*, 15, 131–2.
———. (1982) 'Introduction,' *China Now*, 100, 3.
Seers, D. (1963) 'The Limitations of the Special Case,' *Bulletin of Oxford Institute of Economics and Statistics*, 25(2), 77–98.

———. (1979) 'The Birth, Life and Death of Development Economics,' *Development and Change*, 10, 707–19.
Shove, G.F. (1933) 'Review of Joan Robinson,' *The Economics of Imperfect Competition, Economic Journal*, 43, 657–61.
Social Sciences in China. (1982) 3, 25–6.
Whitehead, D. (1971) 'Review of Robinson (1970g),' *Australian Economic History Review*, 10, 79–81.
Wright, E. (1989a) *The Chinese People Stand Up*. London: BBC.
———. (1989b) 'The Chinese People Stand Up,' *London Calling*, 18, 3.
Wuyts, M. (1981) 'The Mechanization of Present-day Mozambican Agriculture,' *Development and Change*, 12, 1–27.
Yeh, K.C. (1968) 'Capital Formation,' in A. Eckstein, et al. (eds.) *Economic Trends in Communist China*. Edinburgh: University Press, 509–47.

Postscript (2020)

When Joan Robinson visited China for the first time in 1953, it was a backward overpopulated economy. She predicted that as a late socialist industrialiser, China's "vast experiment in modernization" would be historically as important in the second half of the twentieth century as that of the United States in the second half of the nineteenth century. "[T]he Chinese with their innate sense of form in thought and action have a better chance than any other nation to achieve industrialization." The Chinese were free "from the mental contortions of trying to apply Marxism out of the book to their problems. Marx thought of communism as arising out of the explosion of capitalism at its most developed point. China seems to provide the final proof that Communism is not a stage beyond capitalism but a substitute for it."[1]

China today is the second-largest economy of the world in terms of GDP in current US$. It has already left the United States behind in terms of PPP$. Between 1960 and 1976, the year of Mao's death, the size of the economy increased by 2.5 times. Since the start of the socialist market economy in 1978–2018, there has been an enlargement of over 90 times. During the same period, population increased only by less than half times. In the world league tables, it is categorised as an

P. Tahir, *Making Sense of Joan Robinson on China*, Palgrave Studies in the History of Economic Thought, https://doi.org/10.1007/978-3-030-28825-9

upper-middle-income country. There has been a drastic reduction in poverty. Poverty headcount ratio at national poverty line was 17.2 of population in 2010 and has since fallen to 3.1 per cent in 2017. Raising the threshold to $5.50 a day (2011 PPP) shows even more impressive results. From nearly the entire population below this line in 1990, the ratio has been brought down to 27.2 per cent in a matter of 25 years. Income distribution has been problematic, though. The Gini index was high at 32.3 in 1990. It has been declining after peaking to 43.7 in 2010, but at 38.6 in 2015 was still higher than in 1990.[2]

Joan Robinson expected China to beat capitalism at its own game—capital accumulation. The achievements enumerated above were made by a high rate of capital accumulation. Joan Robinson has been widely acknowledged as a great theoretician. *The Economics of Imperfect Competition* (1933) and *The Accumulation of Capital* (1956a) would suffice to make her the first woman Nobel laureate. Her keen interest in the development of Communist China and readiness to go the extra mile to defend not just her own views on the Chinese development but also at times the official Chinese viewpoint is stated to have cost her the honour.[3] The economics profession did not expect an academic of her stature to indulge in pamphleteering. Her own state of mind is reflected in a paragraph that was not included in the foreword of one of her publications on China: "To avoid tedious qualifications, I have written these notes in a positive style, but each statement should be taken with the proviso: 'this is what I was told, or rather: This is what I understood from what 1 was told.'"[4] At the end, she was disillusioned and admitted being starry-eyed. Still, she thought all was not lost: "Whatever illusions I may have had, I feel that the reaction has gone too far. It is absurd to talk of ten wasted years (1966–76) for a great deal of construction went on in that period ... whatever relapse there may be from the ideals of socialism, it will not be a relapse to the misery of old China."[5]

Let it be said that Joan Robinson was not the one who looked for honours. In a man's world and a male-dominated profession, she had to work her way through. She was the only woman in the most distinguished circus of headstrong men, the Cambridge Circus. Every appointment in her career, from a junior assistant to full professor, had to be won the hard way. She had to face gender discrimination at the very entry into the world of academics. She graduated from Girton, but Cambridge had no tradition of awarding degrees to women. Yet at no point in her life did she play the woman card. She was a full-bodied person and an intellectual of unbounded curiosity. She patiently worked on ideas, threw them before the peers and let her mind free to see errors and accept improvement. She was no mathematician, but she had the analytical capability of a mathematician. It was difficult to find fault with the logic of her argument. She was neither an econometrician nor a statistician, but her sense of the ground reality was impeccable.

When it came to Communist China, the same Joan Robinson made unguarded statements, wrote uncritical journalistic articles, defended the indefensible events and fought battles like an activist. How does one make sense of this Joan Robinson? To find an answer, we need to trace the evolution of her thought about economic development of the barely industrialised East.

Before the start of her career as an economist, Joan Robinson had been exposed to economic backwardness, overpopulation and underdevelopment in India towards the end of the 1920s. In 1928, she had returned to Cambridge. She first established herself as a micro-economist with a pioneering work on imperfect competition. Her macroeconomics was shaped by active participation in the Keynesian revolution. Thus, the 1930s witnessed her contributions related to the issues confronting the industrialised West.

To Keynes the worst form of injustice was unemployment and the state had to go against the orthodoxy to intervene and create jobs. He was looking for an alternative to orthodoxy, not capitalism in the industrialised West, and he did provide one with analytical foundations. The rentier aspect of capitalism also worried him. Keynes was no revolutionary and his canvas was limited to highly industrialised economies of the West. Joan Robinson defended and propagated Keynesian policies in the context of the industrialised West to achieve the goal of full employment. None of her writing ever suggested that she was searching for an alternative to capitalism in the developed economies. She looked for alternatives only in the case of developing economies.

Joan Robinson returned to the issues of economic backwardness, overpopulation and underdevelopment after she had established herself in the economics profession. Following Keynes, she had been convinced about the powerful role played by the state in curing mass unemployment. In the 1940s, she turned to understanding Marx and unemployment, socialism, the role of the state, planning and economic dynamics. The debate raging during her stay in India in 1920s had a flavour of Marx's writing on India. But this was the first time she read and re-read Marx. This study led her to the conclusion that the nature of unemployment in the backward economies was Marxian, not Keynesian. It did not arise from demand deficiency but resulted from the available labour running ahead of an already low rate of capital accumulation.

These were her views before visiting China for the first time in 1953. Until her next visit in 1957, she was busy completing her major work, *The Accumulation of Capital*. After developing her insights first into the functioning of prices and the powerful role that the state could play in the economy in boosting employment, studying Marx and visiting China, she moved from the short run to the long run. The main message of the book was similar to Marx: capitalism performed a most effective job of extracting surplus, which was the source of a high rate of capital accumulation.

Joan Robinson was part of an old tradition that thoroughly analysed the dominant ideology called capitalism. The tradition boasts, among others, names like Marx and Rosa Luxemburg. They found the system to be unjust, distributing the large bulk of the social product to the dominant class of capitalists. In the present day and time, the finding has been provided a strong historical and empirical confirmation by Thomas Piketty.[6] Marx looked for an alternative, socialism, communism or by any other name. His analysis was based on the relations of production characterising the industrialised economies. Russia, resource-rich, under-populated but industrially backward, was not on his radar. Soviet communism degenerating into Stalinism was hardly the just alterative he was looking for. But Marx's analysis of the alterative was nothing compared to his analysis of capitalism to inform the campaigners for alternatives.

Joan Robinson found that capitalism did a great job of accumulating capital, but the resulting distribution was inequitable. She was, however, not working for an alternative in the industrialised West. She had already reached the conclusion that the backward economies suffered from

Marxian unemployment. The need here was to boost capital accumulation rather than consumer demand. The first visit to China convinced her that the job of capitalism could be done by the socialist state instead of capitalists. Indeed, the socialist state could beat capitalism at its own game for three reasons. The socialist state could extract greater surplus from agriculture as well as nonagriculture than the capitalists by elimination of the rentier aspect or consumption out of surplus by the capitalists. It will also be more fair and less oppressive than the Soviet-type extraction leading to workers' protests *a'la* Poznan in Poland. In a lecture during her second visit in 1957, she showed the Chinese that an intermediate labour-absorbing technique was possible between the extremes of labour-intensive and capital-intensive techniques. In the other two lectures, she dwelt on the relations between the rate of accumulation and the price level and the usefulness of prices in a planned economy.

Broadly, her viewpoint was similar to the views of the rightists in China—a high rate of capital accumulation, achieved without an intolerable sacrifice of consumption, profit-oriented industrial management to avoid bureaucratic tendency, use of prices with moral supplements, population control, reward by work done and the extraction of agricultural surplus through gradual collectivisation. Inequality, according to her, was associated with private property. With its elimination, she assumed the prevalence of justice in the nonagriculture sector, though the tax-free collective property differentials in agriculture were seen to be a source of inequality. On the whole, she found planning arrangement in China to be working well in industry, but still felt uneasy about the suitability of socialism as a system for agriculture due mainly to the difficulties of organising labour on a large scale.

In her first two visits in 1953 and 1957, she did not show much awareness of political campaigns mounted by Mao. Some elements of the three-antis and five-antis campaigns, particularly that against bureaucratic tendency and land reform, are reflected in her writings for being part of her own thinking. In Joan Robinson's view, the Chinese economy at the end of the first five-year plan (1953–57) was still an overpopulated backward economy, but on the way to overcoming the obstacles to the early stage of industrialisation. The country needed capital accumulation at a humanly possible rate, birth control, some concern for consumer's sovereignty, economic management avoiding the bureaucratic tendency, selective use of prices and some role for moral incentives. These views of her were aligned with what Maoists dubbed as the rightist agenda. Before her second visit in 1957, Mao had made his "Let a hundred flowers bloom" speech in February 1956 that encouraged relatively free intellectual and political expression. By June, the Anti-Rightist Campaign had been unleashed.[7] Oblivious to these developments, she shook hands with Mao on 1 October 1957. One does not see any evidence of her appreciation of the changing political landscape and the challenges to her views on Chinese development.

The Great Leap happened in 1958–61, that is, between her second and third visit. This was a project to squeeze the completion of industrialisation of China from 10–15 years into 3–5 years. Land reform, supported by Joan Robinson, was done away with and collectives, opposed by her for difficulties of supervising labour, were set up. Their counterparts were also created in urban areas. The undernourishment and overexploitation of peasants led to the greatest famine known to human history, and the attempts at backyard steel production were a setback for industrialisation. It was in the aftermath of the Conference of the Seven Thousand in January 1962 that the rightists again took charge of the economy and improved it by revoking the disastrous policies of the Leap. Joan Robinson undertook her third and fourth visits in 1963 and 1964 in these good times. The economy, according to her, had taken a turn for the good. She had doubted the famine stories before her visit and declared them as anti-China propaganda after the visits. At a time of statistical blackout in China, she talked about the Russian famine of 1921. The post-Mao decollectivisation of agriculture had learned from the cruel fact that "the two worst famines of the twentieth century … occurred under collective farming".[8] All along, her own view had been that socialism was for industry, not agriculture.

In 1966, the Cultural Revolution was launched against revisionism, but it was essentially against the rightists who stood exposed during the "hundred flowers". It started with Red Guards attacking teachers and intellectuals. Lin Biao trained rebels attacked the capitalist roaders in the party and the government. Liu Shao-chi was ousted in August 1966. Capitalist roader no. 2, Deng Xiao-ping, was also disgraced. Lin

Biao was made Vice Chairman and heir apparent. As youth preferred fighting to work, economy began to be affected again. Having secured his power, Mao convened the 9th party congress in April 1969. A formal end of the Cultural Revolution was declared.

Joan Robinson's fifth visit was in 1967 with the Cultural Revolution in full swing. She did not think that the economy had taken a turn for the worse. In 1971, Lin Biao's plane crashed. The atmosphere was somewhat relaxed when Joan Robinson arrived for her sixth visit in 1972. According to her, "Chinese policy and political education lay great stress on the moral factor in economic life but they are not starry eyed. They do not rely on moral incentives alone to evoke the heavy toil that a still primitive agriculture needs."[9] The visit was an attempt to see how the economy of China settled down to give effect to the prescription of development emerging from the right-left struggle during the cultural revolution. Joan Robinson had arrived at a time when the campaign against "the ultra-left" and the Lin Biao incident had already taken place, enabling the pragmatic Chou En-lai and the rightists to re-start normal economic activity. So what she witnessed during the visit was again a rightist show. She was told, however, that there was still no distinction being drawn between the Liu line and the ultra-left. One stood for deference, hierarchy and monetary incentives, the other for "Down with everything", yet they are regarded as essentially the same because the consequences of both were equally counterrevolutionary.[10]

Deng was restored in 1973 and made in charge of the army. He was working to wean the system away from the chaotic remnants of the Cultural Revolution and towards the efforts to revive the economy, despite the taunt from Mao: "The weeds of socialism are better than the crops of capitalism."[11] He was arrested after the death of Chou on 8 January 1976 and was freed only after the death of Mao on 9 September 1976. After her only visit to China since Mao, Joan Robinson admitted that she "was relying too much on what 1 have always felt was a remarkable instinct for economic management of the Chinese administration".[12] This volume has argued that this central line or sensible economic management approvingly cited by Joan Robinson was directly associated with the rightist influence, invariably in evidence whenever the Maoists failed in their superhuman campaigns to jump over "the China Walls" of economic and social backwardness.

Joan Robinson analysed and criticised capitalist development in underdeveloped economies. To a lesser extent, this applied to Soviet-type development. For an alternative development model she looked towards China. In the Chinese case, however, she justified more than she analysed and criticised and presented a monolithic view of the Chinese political economy. Like her, the rightists viewed China as a backward overpopulated economy requiring a sustained development of productive forces through central planning supplemented by a regulated use of prices and the market. Compared to the pre-1949 situation, China performed better in terms of price stability, economic growth, health and nutrition. On the questions of population, prices and the market under socialism, and money rent, Joan Robinson was more enthusiastic than the Chinese. She also differed on the absolute necessity of agricultural collectivisation.

In picking up the critical elements of the alternative to capitalism for the developing world, Joan Robinson was more pragmatic than ideological. For example, she advised a socialist government in Sri Lanka not to nationalise the foreign-owned tea plantations. In another example, she told Pakistanis obsessed with having a steel mill as a symbol of self-reliance to trade instead. As a teacher, she believed students from developing countries should be taught analysis, not doctrine. As Keynesian revolution ended "the presumption in favour of laissez-faire," Joan Robinson thought it was "just as important to warn our pupils against new bad mental habits as against the old ones". At the same time, "we must not lose sight of what was valuable in the old orthodoxy. In the U.S.S.R. the laws of supply and demand had to be learned the hard way."[13]

Looking back, how should Joan Robinson's keen interest in extensive writings on China be described? Was she a fellow traveller, the label the China watchers and many in the economics profession put on her? Those who have known her personally or gone through the impressive list of her contributions will vouch that no label sticks. Certainly, she was not a card-carrying member of a communist or socialist party. She was an academic, who was concerned with the lot of the poor in the underdeveloped economies. Curiously, she visited India for a greater number of times than China, in 1920s for about two years and since the 1950s all over India. The Communist-ruled Indian state of Kerala hosted her for a month or two every year during 1972–83. In their essential message, her writings on India were not very dissimilar to the writings on China. But she did not have to face the type of criticism levelled against her works on China. One explanation is that the forces isolating China from the world also encouraged an India-China competition by billing India as the emerging leader of the "free" developing world.[14]

Harcourt, the acknowledged authority on Joan Robinson's person and contribution, says that "Joan Robinson always admitted to a leaven of advocacy in her writings on China because she felt it could do something to offset what she perceived to be the hostility of most other scholars and commentators writing on China. It is true that some of her writings and assessments were far too partial and uncritical, especially during the period of the 'Cultural Revolution' when Mao's influence was at its greatest and the spirit of the (radical) age was a yearning for cult figures and the immediate establishment of utopias. But if we look at the whole body of her writings on China from the early 1950s to the early 1980s, we get a more balanced view."[15]

This is what this volume attempted to do. Based on her critical understanding of the capitalist development in the industrialised world, she had drawn a set of conclusions about an alternative route to development in the underdeveloped world. According to her, a planned socialist economy could generate a greater surplus for capital accumulation by elimination of the consumption of the capitalists. The price mechanism was a feature of capitalism, not prices. A planned use of prices could avoid the mistakes made by the Soviet Union and the overexploitation of workers in Poland. The price incentives would restrain the bureaucratic tendency under socialism and carefully considered moral incentives will prevent gross inequality. In the main, she held on to these views even during the heady days of the Cultural Revolution. She was hoping against hope,[16] like many in the world, including this writer, that the injustice of centuries could be wiped out in decades and the economic progress of decades could be squeezed into years. In the post-Mao period, broadly following the agenda set by Joan Robinson, China did show a double-digit growth for a long time. It is now well on its way to becoming an economic superpower.

In Joan Robinson's view, socialism made it possible to overcome underdevelopment within a generation. The communists had all the power to deal with landlords. What she called "incidentals of development—mass literacy, the freeing of women, the smashing of archaic customs"—come fast under socialism. In early years (1949–52), keeping some role for the private sector was a pragmatic lesson learnt from the Soviet Union that had to step back in its New Economic Policy (NEP). Another lesson from the Soviet experience was to avoid a rush into agricultural collectivisation. Joan Robinson's appreciation of Chinese pragmatism was again witnessed after the fall of Soviet Union in 1991. Just as the Soviet Union rushed into collectivisation in the pre-NEP period, the Russian Federation jumped into marketisation, privatisation and disinvestment with equally disastrous results. The Chinese, on the other hand, liberalised slowly but steadily, and under careful social supervision.

However, Joan Robinson's expectation that socialism, in particular the Chinese socialism, will overcome the inherent tendency of capitalism to be iniquitous did not materialise. Millions have moved out of poverty, but inequality in all its forms—interpersonal, interregional, rural-urban—is rising. As a Chinese scholar Wang Hui underscores, the degeneration of socialist market reform into neoliberal economic reform has undermined the existing social equality.[17] A socially supervised market was expected to preserve existing levels of equality and incrementally improve on it. Socialism, to Joan Robinson, was a substitute for capitalism to achieve a higher rate of capital accumulation by avoiding capitalists' consumption under a different set of rules. Collective saving and investment under these rules would improve distribution. It has not. Income distribution has been problematic. The Gini index was high at 32.3 in 1990. It has been declining after peaking to 43.7 in 2010, but at 38.6 in 2015 was still higher than in 1990. Joan Robinson's expectation about a higher rate of capital accumulation has been realised. Only once in 1962 was the gross capital formation less than 20 per cent of GDP. It has never looked back since, reaching 30 per cent in 1966, 40 per cent in 1985 and 48 per cent in 2011. The latest number relating to 2017 stood at 44 per cent. Population growth is another area where Joan Robinson's expectation came true. From 1.8 per cent in 1960, it came down to 1 per cent by 1997. In 2018, the growth rate was less than half a per cent.

Naturally, the GDP growth per capita has also been the highest ever achieved by any economy. In fact, China is the first economy of the world experiencing double-digit growth per capita for many years. Joan Robinson's conclusion that socialism works more for industry than agriculture is also borne out by the Chinese record. For the entire decade of 2004–14, manufacturing contributed above 30 per cent of GDP. All industry, including manufacturing, during 1970–2018 has contributed over 40 per cent of GDP.[18]

Joan Robinson was an idealist, not an ideologue. Her understanding of the way economies work led her to conclude that the capitalist development was not the route to overcoming poverty, inequality, backwardness and overpopulation in the developing world. She looked towards China, the largest developing economy, for an alternative route to development. However, she readily admitted the gaps in her appreciation of the Chinese reality and her view of socialist development.

Notes

1. Robinson (1954a, 8, b, 125–8).
2. World Bank (2019) https://databank.worldbank.org/home.aspx.
3. Gewirtz, J. (2017) *Unlikely Partners*. Cambridge, MA: Harvard University Press.
4. JVR Collection, 1/15.5. King's College, Cambridge.
5. Robinson (1982, 3).
6. Piketty, T. (2014) *Capital in the Twenty-First Century*. Cambridge, MA: Harvard University Press.
7. Anthropologist Fei Xiaotong organised the "six-professor group", but was declared a rightist in the summer of 1957. Huang Ping, Joshua Muldavin and Xiaojing Lynette, 'Fei Xiaotong,' 134–41, in David Simon (2019) (ed.), *Key Thinkers on Development*. London: Routledge.
8. Nolan (1988, 6).
9. Robinson (1972b, 132).
10. Robinson (1973f, 34).
11. Quoted in Jung Chang and Jon Halliday (2005) *Mao: The Unknown Story*. London: Jonathan Cape, 643.
12. Robinson (1979f, 25).

13. Robinson (1967j, 49–50).
14. For Joan Robinson's engagement with India, see Ashwani Saith (2008), 'Joan Robinson and Indian Planning: An Awkward Relationship,' *Development and Change*, 39, 1115–34.
15. G. C. Harcourt and Prue Kerr (2009) *Joan Robinson*. Houndmills, Basingstoke: Palgrave Macmillan. See also Tahir, Pervez, Harcourt, G. C. and Kerr, P. (2002), 'On Joan Robinson and China,' in Kerr, P. (ed.) with the collaboration of G. C. Harcourt, *Joan Robinson: Critical Assessments of Leading Economists*, Vol. 5, 267–80. London and New York: Routledge.
16. Pervez Tahir (2019) 'Joan Robinson,' 351–6, in David Simon (2019) (ed.), *Key Thinkers on Development*. London: Routledge.
17. Wang Hui (forthcoming) *The Rise of Modern Chinese Thought*. Cambridge, MA: Harvard University Press.
18. World Bank (2019) https://databank.worldbank.org/home.aspx.

References

Unpublished Material

Ajit Singh's letter to the author, 6 January, 1989.
Brammall, C.M. (1989) Inequality and Poverty in Rural China: The Case of Sichuan Province, 1931–1978. Unpublished PhD dissertation, University of Cambridge.
Carl Riskin's letter to the author, 27 February, 1987.
Interview with Lord Kahn, 1 December, 1986.
Interview with Ronald Berger, 20 February, 1987.
JVR Collection, iii/5.1–5.3. King's Modem Archives, King's College Library, Cambridge.
———, 1/15.5. King's College, Cambridge.
K.N. Prasad's letters, 29 September, 1986 and 4 February, 1987.
Liu Minquan, research-in-progress for doctoral dissertation for the University of Oxford.
Sol Adler's letter from Beijing, 30 November, 1986.
Yuming Sheng (1989) Intersectoral Resource Flows in Development Economics with Special Reference to China. Doctoral dissertation, University of Cambridge.

P. Tahir, *Making Sense of Joan Robinson on China*, Palgrave Studies in the History of Economic Thought, https://doi.org/10.1007/978-3-030-28825-9

Published Works

Adelman, I. and D. Sunding. (1989) 'Joan Robinson as a Development Economist,' in G.R. Feiwel (ed.), *Joan Robinson and Modern Economic Theory*, 702–22. London: Macmillan.

Adler, S. (1957) *The Chinese Economy*. London: Routledge and Kegan Paul.

Aird, John S. (1972) 'Population Policy and Demographic Prospects in the People's Republic of China,' in *People's Republic of China: An Economic Assessment. Joint Economic Committee, Congress of the United States (1972)*, 220–331. Washington, DC: U.S. Government Printing Office.

———. (1982) 'Population Studies and Population Policy in China,' *Population and Development Review*, 8(2), 267–97.

Aires, C.E. (1944) *The Theory of Economic Progress*. Chapel Hill: University of North Carolina Press.

Arrow, K.J. (1953) 'Review of Robinson (1951a),' *Econometrica*, 21, 621–3.

Ashbrook, Arthur G. Jr. (1975) 'China: Economic Overview,' in *China: A Reassessment of the Economy. Joint Economic Committee, Congress of the United States. China (1975)*, 20–51. Washington, DC: U.S. Government Printing Office.

Ashton, B., et al. (1984) 'Famine in China, 1958–61,' *Population and Development Review*, 10, 613–45.

Banister, J. (1984) 'Population Policy and Trends in China, 1978–83,' *China Quarterly*, 100, 717–41.

Baran, P. (1957) *The Political Economy of Growth*. New York: Monthly Review Press.

Beitelheim, C. (1958) 'China's Economic Growth,' *Economic Weekly*, 10, 1460–4.

———. (1974) *Cultural Revolution and Industrial Organisation in China*. New York: Monthly Review Press.

———. (1978a) 'Letter of Resignation to the Franco-Chinese Friendship Association,' *Monthly Review*, 30, 9–13.

———. (1978b) 'The Great Leap Backward,' *Monthly Review*, 30, 37–130.

———. (1979) 'China since Mao,' *Monthly Review*, 31, 21–34.

Bell, C. (1969) 'The Debate on China,' *Political Quarterly*, 40, 337–43.

Berger, R. (1974) 'Chinese Economic Planning,' *Broadsheet*, 11, 1–3.

Bowie, R.R. and J.K. Fairbank. (eds.) (1962) *Communist China, 1955–1959: Policy Documents with Analysis*. Cambridge, MA: Harvard University Press.

Braverman, H. (1974) *Labor and Monopoly Capital*. New York: Monthly Review Press.

Bronfenbrenner, M. (1980) 'Review of Robinson (1979c),' *Journal of Economic Literature*, 18, 1581–2.

Bruton, H.J. (1981) 'Review of Robinson (1979b),' *Economic Development and Cultural Change*, 30, 191–6.

Caute, D. (1977) *The Fellow-travellers*. London: Quartet Books.

Chakravarty, S. (1956) 'Time and the Choice of Technique,' *Economic Weekly*, 8, 1097–8.

———. (1983) 'Joan Robinson: An Appreciation,' *Economic and Political Weekly*, 18, 1712–6.

Chen, Chi-yi. (1964) *La Reforme Agraire en Chine Populaire*. The Hague: Mouton.

Ch'en, J. (1969) *Mao*. Englewood Cliffs, NJ: Prentice Hall.

China Quarterly (1973) 'Book Notes,' 56, 798–9.

Churchward, L.G. (1966) 'Review of Robinson (1964h),' *Science and Society*, 30, 100–2.

Coale, A. (1984) *Rapid Population Change in China 1952–1982*. Washington, DC: National Academy of Sciences Press.

Crook, I. and D. Crook. (1965) *The First Years of Yang-yi Commune*. London: Routledge and Kegan Paul.

Dalton, G. (1974) *Economic Systems and Society*. Harmondsworth: Penguin.

Daly, P. (1974) 'China 1974: Growth without Waste,' *China Now*, 45, 3–4.

Dhesi, A.S. (1981) 'Review of Robinson (1979c),' *Kyklos*, 34, 668–70.

Domar, E. (1966) 'The Soviet Collective Farm as a Producer Cooperative,' *American Economic Review*, 56, 734–57.

Dong, F. (1982) 'Relationship between Accumulation and Consumption,' in Xu Dixin, et al. (eds.), *China's Search for Economic Growth*. Beijing: New World Press.

———. (1988) 'Development Theory and Problems of Socialist Developing Economies,' in G. Ranis and T.P. Schultz (eds.), *The State of Development Economics*, 228–53. Oxford: Basil Blackwell.

Donnithorne, A. (1967) *China's Economic System*. New York: Praeger.

Dumonr, R. (1966) *La Chine Surpleuplee, Tiers Monde Affame*. Editions du Seuil.

EcKstein, A. (1966) *Communist China's Economic Growth and Foreign Trade*. New York: McGraw-Hill.

Eclund, G. (1966) *Financing the Chinese Government Budget: Mainland China, 1950–1959*. Chicago: Aldine.

Ellman, M. (1981) 'Agricultural Productivity under Socialism,' *World Development*, 9, 979–89.

Feiwel, G.R. (ed.). (1989) *Joan Robinson and Modern Economic Theory*. London: Macmillan.

Gittings, J. (1985) 'From Brickbats to Bonhomie,' *China Now*, 114, 21–3.

Goldman, M. (1987) 'The Party and the Intellectuals,' in R. Macfarquhar and J.K. Fairbank (eds.), *The Cambridge History of China*, Vol. 14, 218–58. Cambridge: Cambridge University Press.

Government of India. (1956) *Report of the Indian Delegation to China on Agricultural Planning and Techniques*. New Delhi: Government of India Press.

Government of Pakistan (1975) *Economic and Manpower Planning in People's Republic of China: Report of the Delegation of Development Planners and Manpower Experts to People's Republic of China*. Islamabad: Printing Corporation of Pakistan.

Gray, J. (1966) 'China Today: Agrarian Policies,' *Bulletin of the Atomic Scientists*, 22, 32–9.

Griffin, K. and J. Gurley. (1985) 'Radical Analyses of Imperialism, the Third World, and the Transition to Socialism: A Survey Article,' *Journal of Economic Literature*, 23, 1089–143.

Gurley, J.G. (1976) *China's Economy and the Maoist Strategy*. New York: Monthly Review Press.

Han Suyin. (1969) Review of Robinson (1969a). Broadsheet, 6, last page.

Hansen, B. (1975) 'Review of R. Findlay, International Trade and Development Theory in,' *Journal of Development Economics*, 1, 403–4.

Harcourt, G.C. (1982) *The Social Science Imperialists*, P. Kerr (ed.). London: Routledge and Kegan Paul.

———. (1984) 'Harcourt on Robinson,' in H.W. Speigel and W.J. Samuels (eds.), *Contemporary Economists in Perspective*, Vol. 1, Part B. London: Jai Press, 639–54.

Hart, A.T. (1983) 'Joan Robinson: A Personal Note,' *China Now*, 107, 27.

Hayward, J.E.S. (1966) 'Leninizing China and Sinicizing Lenin,' *Political Studies*, 14, 95–9.

Helleiner, G.K. (1980) 'Review of Robinson (1979b),' *Canadian Journal of Economics*, 3, 515–7.

Hou Wenruo. (1981) 'Population Policy,' in Liu Zheng, et al. (eds.), Liu Zheng, et. al. (1981) *China's Population: Problems and Prospects*. Beijing: New World Press , 55–76.

Ishikawa, S. (1975) 'The Chinese Method of Technological Development: The Case of Agricultural Machinery and Implement Industry,' *Developing Economies*, 13, 430–58.

Journal of Contemporary Asia. (1983) Editorial 3, 3–6.

K.A. (1969) 'An Economist Sums Up,' *SACU News*, 6, 5.

Kalecki, M. (1955) 'The Problem of Financing Economic Development,' *Indian Economic Review*, 2(3), 1–22.

———. (1976) *Essays on Developing Economies*. Hassocks, Sussex: Harvester Press.

Karol, K.S. (1975) *The Second Chinese Revolution*. London: Jonathan Cape.

Kerr, C., et al. (1973) *Industrialism and Industrial Man*. Harmondsworth, Middlesex: Penguin.

Kuznets, S. (1966) *Modern Economic Growth: Rate, Structure and Spread*. New Haven: Yale University Press.

Lardy, N.R. (1988) 'Comments on Deng Fureng,' in G. Ranis and T.P. Schultz (eds.), *The State of Development Economics*, 254–9. Oxford: Basil Blackwell.

Leff, N. (1979) 'Entrepreneurship and Economic Development: The Problem Revisited,' *Journal of Economic Literature*, 7, 46–64.

Lippit, V. (1974) *Land Reform and Economic Development in China*. White Plains, NY: International Arts and Science Press.

Liu Minquan. (1989) *Work Incentives in the Production Team in Southern Jiangsu, China, 1960s–70s*. Ld'A-QEH Development Studies Working Paper No. 10, University of Oxford.

———. (1990) *Incentives and Labour Under the Communes in China*. In progress PhD dissertation, University of Oxford.

Liu Suinian and Wu Qungan. (eds.) (1986) *China's Socialist Economy: An Outline History*. Beijing: Beijing Review Press.

Liu Zheng, et al. (1981) *China's Population: Problems and Prospects*. Beijing: New World Press.

Macfarquhar, R. (1974) *The Origins of The Cultural Revolution. 1: Contradictions among the People 1956–1957*. London: Oxford University Press.

———. (1983) *The Origins of The Cultural Revolution. Vol. 2. The Great Leap Forward 1958–1960*. London: Oxford University Press.

Macrae, J. (1977) 'Production, Distribution and Economic Organisation: Income Distribution and Resource Allocation at the Team Level in Rural China,' *Journal of Development Economics*, 4, 365–85.

Mao Tse-tung. (1977a) 'On the Cooperative Transformation of Agriculture [1955],' in *Selected Works*, Vol. 5, 184–207, 1955. Peking: Foreign Languages Press.

———. (1977b) *A Critique of Soviet Economics*. New York: Monthly Review Press.

Marcus, R. (1967) *The Economic Theory of 'Managerial' Capitalism*. London: Macmillan.

———. (1972) 'Is the Corporate Economy a Corporate State?,' *American Economic Review, Papers and Proceedings*, 62, 103–15.

McFarlane, B. (1982) *Radical Economics*. New York: St. Martin's Press.
Monthly Review. (1979) 'Editorial,' 31, 1–19.
Myrdal, G. (1968) *Asian Drama*, Vol. 1–3. London: Allen Lane.
Needham, J. (1965) 'SACU: A Genuine Effort Towards Understanding,' *SACU News*, 1, 1–2.
———. (1978) 'Rise and Fall of the Anti-Intellectual "Gang",' *Nature*, 274, 832–4.
———. (1985) 'The President Looks Back,' *China Now*, 114, 19–20.
Needham, J. and Joan Robinson. (1969) 'Too Much for *The Times*,' *SACU News*, 4, 1–2.
Nolan, P. (1979) 'Inequality of Income between Town and Countryside in the People's Republic of China in the Mid-1950s,' *World Development*, 7, 447–65.
———. (1983a) 'De-collectivisation of Agriculture in China, 1979–82: A Long-term Perspective,' *Economic and Political Weekly*, 8(1395–1406), 1434–41.
———. (1983b) 'De-collectivisation of Agriculture in China,' *Cambridge Journal of Economics*, 7, 381–403.
———. (1983c) *Growth Processes and Distributional Change in a South Chinese Province: The Case of Guangdong*. London: Contemporary China Institute.
———. (1988) *The Political Economy of Collective Farms: An Analysis of China's Post-Mao Reform*. Cambridge: Polity Press.
Nolan, P. and G. White. (1979) 'Socialist Development and Rural Inequality: The Chinese Countryside in the Seventies,' *Journal of Peasant Studies*, 7, 3–48.
———. (1984) 'Urban Bias, Rural Bias or State Bias? Urban-rural Relations in Post-revolutionary China,' *Journal of Development Studies*, 20, 52–81.
Paine, S. (1974) 'Review of *The Chinese Road to Socialism*,' in E.L. Wheelwright and B. McFarlane (eds.), *Conference of Socialist Economists*, Spring, 3, 91–2.
Perkins, D.H. (1975) *China's Modern Economy in Historical Perspective*. Stanford University Press.
———. (1983) 'Research on the Economy of the People's Republic of China: A Survey of the Field,' *Journal of Asian Studies*, 42, 345–78.
———. (1988) 'Reforming China's Economic System, *Journal of Economic Literature*, 26, 601–45.
Perkins, D.H. and S. Yusuf. (1984) *Rural Development in China*. Baltimore: The Johns Hopkins University Press for World Bank.
Phillips, C.S. Jr. (1971) 'The Revival of Cultural Evolution in Social Science Theory,' *Journal of Developing Areas*, 5, 337–70.
Preece, P.F.W. (1968) 'The Priority Given to Heavy Industry in Socialist Economic Planning, *Science and Society*, 32, 288–99.

Raj, K.N. (1956) 'The Indian and Chinese Plans,' *Economic Weekly*, 8, 699–702.
———. (1983) 'Agricultural Growth in India and China,' *Economic and Political Weekly*, 18, 69–75.
Rawsski, T.G. (1975) 'Review of Robinson (1975c),' *China Quarterly*, 64, 756–8.
Reynolds, L.G. (1975) 'China as a Less Developed Economy,' *American Economic Review*, 65(3), 418–28.
Riskin, C. (1975) '"Workers" Incentives in Chinese Industry,' in *China: A Reassessment of the Economy*, 199–224. Congress of the United States, Joint Economic Committee. Washington, DC: U.S. Government Printing Office.
———. (1987) *China's Political Economy: The Quest for Development Since 1949*. New York: Oxford University Press.
Robinson, Joan. (1930) 'Review of H. CLAY *The Problem of Industrial Relations*,' *Political Quarterly*, 1, 293–6.
———. (1937) 'Review of R.H. HALL, *The Economic System in a Socialist State*,' *Cambridge Review*, 58, 289–90.
———. (1942a) *An Essay on Marxian Economics*. London: Macmillan.
———. (1942b) ' Review of L.E. Hubbard, *Soviet Labour and Industry*,' *Cambridge Review*, 63, 348–9.
———. (1943a) 'Review of Schumpeter (1943),' *Economic Journal*, 53, 381–3.
———. (1943b) *The Future of Industry*. London: Fredrick Muller.
———. (1943c) *Private Enterprise or Public Control*. London: The English Universities Press.
———. (1943d) *The Problem of Full Employment*. London: The Workers' Educational Association and Workers' Educational Trade Union Committee.
———. (1949) 'Theory of Planning,' Review of M. Dobb. *Soviet Economic Development Since 1917, Soviet Studies*, 1, 60–4.
———. (1951a) *Collected Economic Papers*, Vol. l. Oxford: Basil Blackwell.
———. (1951b) 'Preparation for War,' Reprinted from *Cambridge Today* in *Monthly Review*, 3, 194–5.
———. (1952a) 'Theory and Practice of Planning,' Review of C. Bettelheim, *Problemes Theoriques et Pratiques de La Planification, Soviet Studies*, 4, 53–8.
———. (1952b) *Conference Sketch Book*. Cambridge: Heifer.
———. (1953a) *On Re-reading Marx*. Cambridge: Students' Bookshops.
———. (1953b) 'On Trade with Russia,' Letter to *The Times*, 1 September, 7.
———. (1953c) 'East-West Trade,' Letter to *The Times*, 15 September, 7.
———. (1953d) 'A Mission to Moscow,' Letter to *The Economist*, 28 November, 655.
———. (1953e) Letter to *The Economist*, 5 December, 742.

———. (1954a) *Letters from a Visitor to China*. Cambridge: Students' Bookshops.
———. (1954b) 'Britain and China,' *Nation*, 179, 125–8.
———. (1955a) 'A Theory of Long-run Development,' *Economic Review*, October 1955a, 6, 382–5.
———. (1955b) *Marx, Marshall and Keynes*. Delhi: Delhi School of Economics, Occasional Paper No. 9.
———. (1956a) *The Accumulation of Capital* 1st ed. London: Macmillan.
———. (1956b) 'Unemployment and the Second Plan,' *Capital*, Annual Supplement, 7–9. Reprinted in Robinson (1965a), 182–91.
———. (1956c) 'Employment and the Plan,' *Economic Weekly*, 8, 355–6.
———. (1956d) 'The Choice of Techniques,' *Economic Weekly*, 8, 715–18.
———. (1956e) 'Time and the Choice of Technique,' Comment on Chakravarty (1956), *Economic Weekly*, 8, 1333.
———. (1956f) 'British-Soviet Trade Prospects,' *British-Soviet Friendship*, October.
———. (1957a) 'The Policy of Backward Nations. Review of BARAN (1957),' *Nation*, 184, 485–6.
———. (1957b) 'Clues to History,' Rejoinder to Paul Sweezy. *Nation*, 185, opp. L.
———. (1957c) 'Notes on the Theory of Economic Development,' *Annales de la Faculté de Droit de Liège*. Also in Robinson (1960a), *Collected Economic Papers*, Vol. 2. Oxford: Basil Blackwell. 88–113.
———. (1957d) 'What Remains of Marxism,' in Robinson (1965a), *Collected Economic Papers*, Vol. 3. Oxford: Basil Blackwell, 158–66.
———. (1957e) 'The Indian Mixture,' Review of M. Zinkin. *Development for free Asia, New Statesman and Nation*, 54, 844–5.
———. (1957f) 'Choice of Technique,' Letter to *Economic Weekly*, 9, 537.
———. (1958a) 'Birth Control in China,' *New Statesman and Nation*, 55, 66–7.
———. (1958b) 'Some Reflections on the Philosophy of Prices,' *Manchester School of Economics and Social Studies*, 26, 116–35.
———. (1959) 'Economic Possibilities of Ceylon,' in *Papers by Visiting Economists*, 38–71. Colombo: National Planning Council.
———. (1960a) *Collected Economic Papers*, Vol. 2. Oxford: Basil Blackwell.
———. (1960b) 'Population and Development,' *Pakistan Economic Journal*, 10, 1–7.
———. (1960c) *Exercises in Economic Analysis*. London: Macmillan.

———. (1960d) 'Review of T.T. Hughes and D.E.T. Luard,' *The Economic Development of Communist China, Economic Journal*, 70, 409–10.
———. (1960e) 'The Philosophy of Prices,' in Robinson, 1960a, 27–48.
———. (1960f) 'East-West Trade,' Letter to *The Economist*, 16 January, 195.
———. (1961a) 'From the United States to Cuba,' *Listener*, 66, 265–7, 80.
———. (1961b) 'Review of S. Tsuru (ed.),' *Has Capitalism Changed? Monthly Review*, 13, 265–71.
———. (1962a) *Economic Philosophy*. London: C.A. Watts.
———. (1962b) 'Review of E.S. Kirby (ed.),' *Contemporary China. Economic Journal*, 72, 734.
———. (1963a) 'Public and Private Enterprise,' *Applied Economic Papers*, 1–12.
———. (1963b) 'Review of G. Maynard,' *Economic Development and the Price Level, Economic Journal*, 73, 299–300.
———. (1963c) 'The Chinese View,' *Seminar*, 50, 44–6.
———. (1963d) 'Are We Exerting Ourselves Enough? Compete with Chinese,' *Yojana*, 7, 7–8.
———. (1964a) 'Communes in China,' *Listener*, 71, 177–89.
———. (1964b) 'Notes from China,' *Economic Weekly*, 16, 195–203.
———. (1964c) 'A British Economist on Chinese Communes,' *Eastern Horizon*, 3, 6–11.
———. (1964d) 'Chinese Agricultural Communes,' *Coexistence*, 1, 1–6.
———. (1964e) 'The Chinese Communes,' *Political Quarterly*, 35, 285–97.
———. (1964f) 'The Chinese Point of View,' *International Affairs*, 40, 232–44.
———. (1964g) 'Prospects for China,' *New Scientist*, 22, 756.
———. (1964h) *Notes from China*. Oxford: Basil Blackwell.
———. (1964i) 'Planning for Economic Development,' *Trade Journal* (Pakistan), June–July, 5–7.
———. (1964j) 'Review of S.H. Chou,' *The Chinese Inflation, 1937–1949, Economic Journal*, 74, 680–1.
———. (1964k) 'India, Wake Up!,' *Economic Weekly*, 16, 1917–20.
———. (1964l) 'Consumer's Sovereignty in a Planned Economy,' in *On Political Economy and Econometrics: Essays in Honour of Oskar Lange*. Oxford: Pergman Press. Also in Robinson (I965a), 70–81.
———. (1964m) 'Review of H.G. Shaffer (ed.),' *The Soviet Economy. Cambridge Review*, 85, 491–2.
———. (1965a) *Collected Economic Papers*, Vol. 3. Oxford: Basil Blackwell.
———. (1965b) 'China, 1963: The Communes,' in Robinson (1965a), 192–206.
———. (1965c) 'What's New in China?' *Eastern Horizon*, 4, 11–5.

———. (1965d) 'Korean Miracle,' *Monthly Review*, 16 (9), 541–9.
———. (1965e) 'Cuba, 1965,' *Economic Weekly*, 17, 1341–5.
———. (1965f) Review of Ta-chung Liu and Kung-chia Yeh, *The Economy of Chinese Mainland: National Income and Economic Development, 1933–1959. Economic Journal*, 75, 604.
———. (1965g) 'Economic Principles in China,' Review of C. Bettelheim, et al., *Construction du Socialisme en Chine, Broadsheet*, 2, 1–3.
———. (1965h) Review of P.J.D. Wiles, *The Political Economy of Communism*, in Robinson, (1965a), 82–91.
———. (1966a) 'Review of Walker (1965),' *International Affairs*, 42, 159–60.
———. (1966b) 'Cuba—1965,' *Monthly Review*, 17, 10–18.
———. (1966c) 'China Today: The Organisation of Agriculture,' *Bulletin of the Atomic Scientists*, 22, 28–32.
———. (1966d) 'Organisation of Agriculture,' in R. Adams (ed.), *Contemporary China*. London: Peter Owen.
———. (1966e) 'Reviews of Chen Chi-yi, *La Reforme Agraire en Chine Populaire;* Yuan-li Wu. *The Steel Industry In Communist China*,' *International Affairs*, July 42, 546–8.
———. (1966f) 'Review of C. Bettelheim, et al., La Construction du Socialisme en Chine,' *Coexistence*, 3, 105–7.
———. (1966g) 'The Communes and the Great Leap Forward,' Reviews of Crook and Crook (1965); Dumont (1966). *New Left Review*, 37, 69–72.
———. (1966h) *Economics: An Awkward Corner*. London: George Allen and Unwin.
———. (1967a) 'Contribution to Sanity,' Letter. *Economic and Political Weekly*, 2, 111.
———. (1967b) 'The Soviet Collective Farm as a Producer Cooperative: Comment,' *American Economic Review*, 57(1), 222–3.
———. (1967c) 'Reviews of Yuan-li Wu, *The Economy of Communist China*, D.H. Perkins *Market Control and Planning in Communist China*; J.L. Buck, L. Dawson and Yuan-li Wu, *Food and Agriculture in Communist China*.' *International Affairs*, 43, 192–3.
———. (1967d) 'Reviews of A.N. Young, *China's Wartime Finance and Inflation, 1937–1945, and Foreign Investment*; Chi-ming Hou, *Economic Development in China, 1840–1937*,' *International Affairs*, 43, 404–6.
———. (1967e) 'Review of H. P. Ortisch,' *Eyewitness in China, International Affairs*, 43, 611–2.
———. (1967f) 'Review of *The Awakening of China, 1793–1949*,' *International Affairs*, 43, 797.

———. (1967g) 'The Economic Reforms,' *Monthly Review*, 19, 45–50.
———. (1967h) 'Socialist Affluence,' in C.H. Feinstein (ed.), *Socialism, Capitalism and Economic Growth: Essays in Honour of Maurice Dobb*. London: Cambridge University Press. Also in Robinson, (1973a), 33–47.
———. (1967i) 'The Chinese Cultural Revolution,' *Now*, 22 December.
———. (1967j) 'Opening Remarks,' in K. Martin and John Knapp (eds.), *The Teaching of Development Economics*. London: Frank Cass, 149–50.
———. (1967k) 'Growth and the Theory of Distribution,' *Annals of Pubic and Co-operative Economics*, 38(1), 3–7.
———. (1968a) 'Review of Jan Myrdal,' *Report from a Chinese Village, International Affairs*, 44, 152–3.
———. (1968b) 'Intensive Look at China,' *SACU News*, 3, 1–5.
———. (1968c) 'The Cultural Revolution in China,' *International Affairs*, 44, 214–27.
———. (1968d) 'Reply to Sussex Internationalists' Attack, *SACU News*, 3, 5.
———. (1968e) 'China Today: Economic Organisation,' *Journal of the Royal Society of Arts*, 116, 683–93.
———. (1968f) 'The Poverty of Nations. Review of Myrdal (1968),' *Listener*, 80, 509–10, 517.
———. (1968g) 'One Quarter of Mankind,' *Canadian Forum*, 48, 150. 'Review of Myrdal,' *Cambridge Quarterly*, 3, 381–9.
———. (1968h) 'The Decentralised Society. Review of A. Donnithorne,' *China's Economic System, SACU News*, 5.
———. (1969a) *The Cultural Revolution in China*. Harmondsworth, Middlesex: Penguin Books.
———. (1969b) 'Ten Years of Communes,' *Broadsheet*, 6, 3.
———. (1969c) 'Review of Myrdal (1968),' *Canadian Dimension*, 5, 27–30.
———. (1969d) 'India and China: A Comparison,' *Listener*, 82, 816–18.
———. (1969e) 'Preface,' in N. Brunner (ed.), *China's Economy*. London: Anglo-Chinese Educational Institute, 1–2.
———. (1969f) Letter to *Tribune*, 24 January.
———. (1970a) 'Reply to A.J. Watson,' *China Now*, 2, 4.
———. (1970b) Reviews of K. Buchanan, *The Transformation of the Chinese Earth*; T.R. Tregear, *Economic Geography of China, Broadsheet*, 7, last page.
———. (1970c) 'Society and Economics in China Today,' in R. Jungk, et al., *China and the West: Mankind Evolving*. London: Granstone Press, 35–47.
———. (1970d) 'Chinese Economic Policy,' *Studium Generale*, 23, 1267–74.
———. (1970e) 'Chinese Economic Policy: Prescription for Development,' *China Now*, 4, 5–8.

———. (1970f) 'Foreword,' in E.L. Wheelwright and B. McFarlane (eds.), *The Chinese Road to Socialism*. New York: Monthly Review Press.
———. (1970g) *Freedom and Necessity*. London: George Allen and Unwin.
———. (1971a) 'Chinese Economic Policy,' in J. Needham, et al., *Hand and Brain in China and Other Essays*. London: Anglo-Chinese Educational Institute, 19–27.
———. (1971b) 'Something to Live for. Review of J. Myrdal and G. Kessle,' *The Revolution Continued New Statesman*, 81, 631–3.
———. (1972a) 'For Use, Not for Profit,' *Eastern Horizon*, 11, 6–15.
———. (1972b) 'Through Western Spectacles,' Reviews of K. Mehnert, *China Today*; Terrill (1972); and K. Ling, *Red Guard, Spectator*, 7522, 321.
———. (1973a) *Collected Economic Papers*, Vol. 4. Oxford: Basil Blackwell.
———. (1973b) 'Ideology and Analysis,' in Robinson (1979a), *Collected Economic Papers*, Vol. 5. Oxford: Basil Blackwell, 254–61.
———. (1973c) 'Chinese Agricultural Communes,' in Wilber, C.K. (ed.) (1973). *The Political Economy of Development and Underdevelopment*. New York: Random House, Wilber (1973), 209–15. Also 2nd ed. 1979.
———. (1973d) 'Structure of Management,' *China Now*, 29, 10–11.
———. (1973e) 'Planning and Management in China Today,' *Cambridge Review*, 94, 106–20.
———. (1973f) *Economic Management in China, 1972*. London: Anglo-Chinese Educational Institute.
———. (1973g) 'Review of W. Brus,' *The Market in a Socialist Economy, Economic Journal*, 83, 258–60.
———. (1974a) 'Introduction' to *Selected Economic Writings*. Bombay: Oxford University Press, ix–xiii.
———. (1974b) 'Inflation West and East,' in Robinson (1979a), *Collected Economic Papers*, Vol. 5, 215–21. Oxford: Basil Blackwell.
———. (1974c) 'Achievements of a Generation,' *China Now*, 45, 2–3.
———. (1974d) 'Two Revolutions,' *Broadsheet*, 11, 4.
———. (1974e) 'Markets,' in *Encyclopaedia Britannica*, 15th ed. An expanded version in Robinson (1979a), 146–67.
———. (1974f) 'On the Pollyanna of Economic Growth. Review of W. Beckerman,' *In Defence of Economic Growth, Spectator*, 7619, 19–20.
———. (1974g) 'False Development,' Review of J. White, *The Politics of Foreign Aid, Spectator*, 7631, 401–2.
———. (1974h) "Inflation and Stabilisation: A Neo-Keynesian View,' *Spectator*, 19 October 1974h, 7634, 488–9.

———. (1975a) 'Introduction 1974: Reflections and Reminiscences,' in *Collected Economic Papers*, Vol. 2, 2nd ed. Oxford: Basil Blackwell, iii–xii.
———. (1975b) 'Introduction 1974: Comments and Explanations,' in *Collected Economic Papers*, Vol. 3, 2nd ed. Oxford: Basil Blackwell, iii–xiv.
———. (1975c) *Economic Management in China*. 2nd ed. London: Anglo-Chinese Educational Institute.
———. (1975d) 'Foreword,' in P. Mauger et al., *Education in China*. London: Anglo-Chinese Educational Institute, 1–2.
———. (1975e) Review of Leslie R. Marchant,' *To Phoenix Seat: An Introductory Study of Maoism and the Chinese Communist Quest for a Paradise on Earth*, *History*, 60, 272–3.
———. (1975f) 'National Minorities in Yunnan,' *Eastern Horizon*, 14, 32–43.
———. (1975g) 'In the Deep Southwest,' *New China Magazine*, 1, 721–3.
———. (1975h) 'Hsishuang Parma,' *China Now*, 55, 10–11, 15–16.
———. (1975i) 'The Fall of Lin Piao.' Review of P. Worsley, *Inside China*; K.S. Karol, *The Second Chinese Evolution, Spectator*, 7677, 217.
———. (1976a) 'Review of J.K. Fairbank, et al.,' *East Asia: Tradition and Transformation, Journal of Royal Asiatic Society* 76, 91–2.
———. (1976b) 'An Eyewitness Account of the Cultural Revolution,' Review of John and Elsie Collier, *China's Socialist Revolution, Monthly Review*, 28, 50–1.
———. (1976c) 'Introduction,' Kalecki, M. (1976) *Essays on Developing Economies*. Hassocks, Sussex: Harvester Press.
———. (1976d) 'Walled in,' Review of E.S. Kirby, *Russian Studies of China, Spectator*, 7699, 17.
———. (1977a) 'Employment and the Choice of Technique,' in K.S. Krishnaswamy et al., (ed.) *Society and Change*. Bombay: Oxford University Press, 156–69.
———. (1977b) *Reports from China, 1953–76*. London: Anglo-Chinese Educational Institute.
———. (1977c) 'Review of E. Brun and J. Hersh. *Socialist Korea: A Case Study in the Strategy of Economic Development*,' *Monthly Review* 29, 60–2.
———. (1977d) 'Guidelines of Orthodox Economics,' *Journal of Contemporary Asia*, 7, 22–6.
———. (1977e) 'Education,' *Social Scientist*, 5, 131–7.
———. (1978a) *Contributions to Modern Economics*. Oxford: Basil Blackwell.
———. (1978b) 'Formalism versus Dogma,' Review of I. Steedman, *Marx after Sraffa. Journal of Contemporary Asia*, 8, 381–4.

———. (1978c) 'China 1978: Comments on Bettelheim,' *China Now*, 80, 4–7.
———. (1978d) 'Review of Mao Tse-tung (1977),' *China Now*, 80, 26–7.
———. (1978e) 'Morality and Economics,' *Challenge*, 21, 62–4.
———. (1979a) *Collected Economic Papers*, Vol. 5. Oxford: Basil Blackwell.
———. (1979b) *Aspects of Development and Underdevelopment*. Cambridge: Cambridge University Press.
———. (1979c) 'Surplus Value and Profits: The Rectification of Names,' *Development and Change*, 10, 693–5.
———. (1979d) 'Review of MAO (1977),' *Monthly Review*, 30, 52–3.
———. (1979e) 'China since Mao,' *Monthly Review*, 31, 48–56.
———. (1979f) 'The Pros and Cons,' *China Now*, 86, 25–6.
———. (1980a) 'Review of H. Chenery,' *Structural Change and Development Policy, Journal of Developing Areas*, 15, 131–2.
———. (1980b) Review of N. Maxwell (ed.) *China's Road to Development, Broadsheet*, 17, last page.
———. (1981) Reprint of Robinson (1979b) *Aspects of Development and Underdevelopment*. Cambridge: Cambridge University Press.
———. (1982) 'Introduction,' *China Now*, 100, 3.
Robinson, Joan and S. Adler. (1958) *China: An Economic Perspective*. London: Fabian International Bureau, Fabian Tract No. 314.
Robinson, Joan and R. Berger. (1961) 'Thinking about China: The Economic Impact of Communism,' *Listener*, 2 February 1961, 65, 220–2.
Robinson, Joan and J. Eatwell. (1973) *An Introduction to Modern Economics*. London: McGraw-Hill.
Roll, C.R. (1974) *The Distribution of Rural Income in China: A Comparison of the 1930s and the 1950s*. Doctoral dissertation, Harvard University, Cambridge, MA.
Sauvy, A. (1957), 'La Population de la Chine,' *Population*, 12, 695–706.
Schumpeter, J.A. (1943) *Capitalism, Socialism and Democracy*. London: Allen and Unwin.
———. (1968) *Ideology and Organisation in Communist China*. Berkeley: University of California Press.
Seers, D. (1963) 'The Limitations of the Special Case,' *Bulletin of Oxford Institute of Economics and Statistics*, 25(2), 77–98.
———. (1979) 'The Birth, Life and Death of Development Economics,' *Development and Change*, 10, 707–19.
Shove, G.F. (1933) 'Review of Joan Robinson,' *The Economics of Imperfect Competition, Economic Journal*, 43, 657–61.

Singh, A. (1979) 'The "Basic Needs" Approach to Development vs the New International Order: The Significance of Third World Industrialisation,' *World Development*, 7, 585–606.

Skinner, G.W. (1965) 'Marketing and Social Structure in China, Part III,' *Journal of Asian Studies*, 24, 363–99.

Snow, E. (1938) *Red Star Over China*. New York: Random House. Reprinted 1968, 1978.

Social Sciences in China. (1982) 3, 25–6.

Terrill, R. (1972) *800,000,000: The Real China*. London: Heinemann.

Thomson, G. (1971) *From Marx to Mao*. London: China Policy Study Group.

Tian Xueyuan. (1981) 'A Survey of Population Growth since 1949,' in Liu Zheng, et al., 32–54.

Tintner, G. and P. Peek. (1976) 'Marginalism and Linear Economics East and West,' *History of Political Economy*, 8, 367–79.

Turner, M.S. (1989) *Joan Robinson and the Americans*. Armonk, NY: M.E. Sharpe.

Vogel, E.F. (1969) *Canton under Communism: Programs and Politics in a Provincial Capital, 1949–1968*. Cambridge, MA: Harvard University Press.

Walker, K.R. (1965) *Planning in Chinese Agriculture*. Chicago: Aldine.

———. (1966) 'Collectivisation in Retrospect: The "Socialist Hightide" of Autumn 1955–Spring 1956,' *China Quarterly*, 26, 1–43.

Ward, B. (1958) 'The Firm in Illyria: Market Syndicalism,' *American Economic Review*, 48, 566–89.

Watson, A.J. (1969) 'Review of Robinson (1969a),' *China Quarterly*, 40, 163–4.

———. (1970) 'The Cultural Revolution: Two Views,' *China Now*, 2, 3–4.

White, L.T. (1989) *Politics of Chaos: The Organisational Causes of Violence in China's Cultural Revolution*. Princeton: Princeton University Press.

Whitehead, D. (1971) 'Review of Robinson (1970g),' *Australian Economic History Review*, 10, 79–81.

Wilber, C.K. (ed.) (1973) *The Political Economy of Development and Underdevelopment*. New York: Random House. Also 2nd ed. 1979.

Wright, E. (1989a) *The Chinese People Stand Up*. London: BBC.

———. (1989b) 'The Chinese People Stand Up,' *London Calling*, 18, 3.

Wuyts, M. (1981) 'The Mechanization of Present-day Mozambican Agriculture,' *Development and Change*, 12, 1–27.

Yeh, K.C. (1968) 'Capital Formation,' in A. Eckstein, et al. (eds.) *Economic Trends in Communist China*. Edinburgh: University Press, 509–47.

Zhong, C.Z. (1961) 'On Differential Rent in China's Rural Communes,' *Red Flag*, 1 December.

Index[1]

[1] Note: Page numbers followed by 'n' refer to notes.

P. Tahir, *Making Sense of Joan Robinson on China*, Palgrave Studies in the History of Economic Thought, https://doi.org/10.1007/978-3-030-28825-9

C

The manufacturer's authorised representative in the EU is Springer Nature Customer Service Centre GmbH, Europaplatz 3, 69115 Heidelberg, Germany. If you have any concerns regarding our products, please contact ProductSafety@springernature.com

Printed and bound by CPI Group (UK) Ltd, Croydon, CR0 4YY
05/10/2026
02228143-0001